To

We'll

Deb, Joe, Willie & Maddie

Victoria's BEST BARGAINS

ANNE GARBER

JOHN T.D. KEYES

$ERIOUS PUBLISHING

First edition, August 1994
Cover and book design by Dan Murphy
Back cover photography by Kit (C.D.) Johnson
Typesetting by The Typeworks, Vancouver

Serious Publishing
7249 Waverley Avenue
Burnaby, B.C. V5J 4A7
phone: (604) 879-0321
fax: (604) 875-0007

Printed in Canada on recycled paper
by Kromar Printing, Winnipeg

Canadian Cataloguing in Publication Data

Garber, Anne
Victoria's best bargains

Includes index.
ISBN 0-9695187-4-9

1. Shopping—British Columbia—Victoria Metropolitan Area—Directories. 2. Service industries—British Columbia—Victoria Metropolitan Area—Directories. I. Keyes, John T. D., 1952–
II. Title.
TX337.C22V52 1994 381'.45'0002571128 C94-910576-7

To my close friends, my wonderful children and my favourite man—you all know *who you are.*

—A.G.

To my parents, Gordon and Mary Keyes, because they should be living here.

—J.T.D.K.

Please note: Prices, hours and even proprietors of the stores, services and restaurants mentioned herein are subject to change, and therefore specific details cannot be guaranteed. Please call ahead to assure you will not be disappointed. Inclusion in this book is not to be considered an endorsement of goods, stores, shopping areas or restaurants by the authors or publisher. No remuneration, goods or services have been tendered to or accepted by the authors or publisher in return for inclusion or favourable comment in this book.

Acknowledgements: We are grateful for the help, support and kind wishes of Deirdre Campbell; Cary Corbeil; Heather-Elayne Day; Celia Duthie; Lorraine Gannon; Becky Johnson; Kit Johnson; Ted Johnson; Norman Levi; Ezra, Peter & Sheila Maidstone; Kerry Moore; Helen & Bob Pearce (and Helen's students); Harry Roet; Marcia Simenoff; Terry Spence; Shelagh Stanley; James & Jan Townsend; Marilyn Wargo; and Ray Wargo.

CONTENTS

INTRODUCTION

Welcome to the premier edition of *Victoria's Best Bargains.* I know Victoria has been waiting for this book, because as long as I've been writing the *Vancouver Super Shopper*—over a decade now—Victoria residents have been hounding me to do one for them.

Over the past eleven years, hunting out the "real" deals has become a way of life for me (and everyone else I know). As we all are aware, Victoria bargain-seekers face a bigger challenge than do their counterparts on the mainland. It was my good fortune to convince Victoria homeowner John Keyes to do this book with me, because he revealed the Island's secrets to me in a way I could never have discovered on my own.

We haven't gone as far as Nanaimo for this edition, since we figured that those who already know about the great deals at *Costco* have found the direct route to it.

This book tells you where to find the best local buys. The index we've provided will help you find the specific items you need quickly. I must confess I keep my own copy in my car and refer to it constantly—and the index DOES work!

Even the best directory of bargain stores can only point you in the right direction; it can't tell you how to choose between trash and treasure. With that disclaimer, here are Mother Garber's patented Top Ten Tips to help guide you:

1. Never assume anything is a bargain. Bargains and non-bargains are often stocked side by side. Anyone can slap the word "discount" on his store—sometimes it just ain't so.

2. Shop seasonally. You'll find the best sales in July—and naturally the savings on many items abound right after Christmas and the New Year. Candy discounts are best after Easter, Valentine's Day and Christmas.

3. Learn to develop a feel for quality. The best-informed consumer stands the best chance of saving money. Buying a low-grade product at a low pricc is no savings unless you are fully aware of what you are getting. Reading sales flyers is informative, and keeping Christmas catalogues until the next year helps you measure price changes and figure out when a bargain really is a bargain.

4. Know your prices. This will stand you in good stead when you purchase staple items. Plan to stock up when you find a genuine bargain. A year's supply of anything bought at bargain rates will make you feel smug for the full 12 months when you watch inflation steadily push prices up.

5. Be willing to question the asking price, especially if you feel it's too high or if you are contemplating a large order. Dickering can be surprisingly profitable in these days of slow retail trade.

6. Don't hesitate to return merchandise if store policy permits. Nothing will make you feel worse about bargain shopping than ending up with a lot of unnecessary items you don't really need. Similarly, if you're buying goods sold as "first-quality" and you discover a flaw, return them—but always inquire about the store's returns policy BEFORE YOU BUY.

7. Provide feedback. This doesn't mean complain about every-

thing, including the weather. It means express your dissatisfaction if an item is over-priced or shoddy, but also be prepared to compliment the owner if service is friendly, prices fair or a sale is spectacular.

8. Tell your friends. Surprisingly, lots of business at bargain stores does not drive prices up. Quite the contrary, if you want to find these stores still operating a year from now, send them all the customers you can.

9. Pay cash whenever possible. Ask if you can get a discount for paying cash. Retailers pay for the privilege of taking Visa or MasterCard, so they may be willing to discount your cash purchase about 5%. Visitors from the United States should also remember to enquire about the exchange rate (if it's not posted), prior to selecting goods—negotiations may be tricker after you've found something you can't live without. And the Debit card (InterAc) is new on the scene—even grocery stores are using the system.

10. Check before buying. Check out those warranties, guarantees, service contracts and delivery charges before making your purchase.

It's amazing how difficult it is to keep this sort of publication current. Some places were moving locations, swapping owners or even changing name as we went to press, so it's a safe bet that nothing stays the same for long.

Sometimes you have to play detective and call Directory Assistance to see if there is a new listing for the store elsewhere. Mentioning prices is precarious in these economic times, but sometimes we've quoted prices anyway, merely as a guideline. It's just an observation, but it seems to me that recent price changes merely reflect the minimal upward gains in cost of living—less than 5% on average. Unfortunately, experience shows that even the best bargain spot is no more immune to the effects of inflation than we are.

For those of you who have never dealt with used and consignment outlets, I suggest you consider the following: [1] Even if you don't want to buy, you can sell or consign and make a profit on goods you no longer want; and [2] I believe the quality of general consumer goods has not improved substantially over time, so it may be true that "older is better." Recycling is a revolt against planned obsolescence as well as inflation.

Other sources of inexpensive goods are the classifieds in the daily newspapers, ads in local community papers and of course, *The Buy and Sell.* I was surprised to discover that a very good way to purchase bargains was to advertise in "Miscellaneous Wanted To Buy" in both *The Times Colonist* and *Monday.* That means *you* get all the calls, and you can pick and choose the best prices. This ploy is particularly effective when searching for furniture, garden tools, ladders, tools and machinery.

You might also want to explore *The Advantage Exchange Group,* a local network buying group which you can join. For membership details, write Reed Sumida at Box 5487, Stn B, Victoria V8R 6S4, or call 595-2810.

If we've failed to discover your "best buy in town" and you are willing to share it with others, please drop us a line at *Serious Publishing,* 7249 Waverley Ave., Burnaby, BC, V5J 4A7, send Anne Garber a note c/o *The Province,* 2250 Granville St., Vancouver BC, V6H 3G2, send John Keyes a missive at 1157 Empress Ave., Victoria V8T 1P3, or fax the info to (604) 875-0007 or (604) 433-5594.

Meanwhile, why are you sitting there reading? Get out there and take advantage of those deals!

Anne Garber
August, 1994

HOW TO USE THIS BOOK

You'll find both a table of contents (at the front) and an alphabetical index (by store name and type of item) in the back, which make hunting for some specific need easier. If you know the name of the store you're seeking—obviously—use the index. If you're shopping around for, say, bunk beds or a new washing machine, locate the subject category and call as many places as you can, to compare prices.

Unless otherwise noted, addresses given are in Greater Victoria. In the entries, we've included hours of operation (where applicable), address and phone numbers, and even fax numbers. For places in Victoria proper, we've occasionally mentioned an area (Fernwood, Oak Bay, Esquimalt), which may help you find your bearings (and the place in question) more easily.

In places where parking is a problem, we've tried to give you some hints about how your "parking karma" might pay off. Note that areas like Sidney (10 minute signs mean just that), and the streets around Market Square, are always problematic for parking, and be cautious in those particular neighbourhoods, because illegally parked cars are promptly ticketed all day long! All of the suburban malls offer free parking.

We mention whether the store takes cash only, cheques (they usually won't accept out-of-town or out-of-province cheques), or if they take credit cards, which means Visa, MasterCard and sometimes En Route, Diner's Club and American Express. If the shop takes Visa only (which does happen), we've tried to note that, too. Some stores now take the debit card (InterAc), and Travellers cheques are acceptable everywhere, just like cash.

As we go to press, we're aware that some businesses will have moved, closed, acquired new personnel, changed their hours or changed their names by the time you read this book. In order to avoid disappointment—*please*—call before you head out on a cross-town shopping adventure.

1. RESTAURANT DEALS

GENERAL LISTINGS

Sticking with our notion that value-for-money is better than simply the lowest price (though food definitely tastes better when it costs less), we've selected these Victoria restaurants to help fill your tummies without emptying your wallets.

ALI BABA PIZZA
1011 Blanshard St (385-6666)
Hours: Mon–Th 11 a.m.–midnight; Fri 11 a.m.–2 a.m.; Sat noon–2 a.m.; Sun noon–10

You can choose one of two 2-for-1 deals here: Either order two pizzas for the price of one, or can ask for double toppings on one pie. One tantalizing menu item is "The Ultimate"—which allows you to load on "every topping we have except what you don't like." With 23 toppings available, this is a great deal (small

$18.80; med. $23.05; large $27.30). If you want a thin crust, you have to ask for it specifically. Caters to parties; prices on request. Free delivery.

Credit cards

BARB'S PLACE FISH 'N CHIPS
Fisherman's Wharf, 310 St. Lawrence St (384-6515)
Hours: Daily 8:30 a.m. until sunset

You can't miss the happy crowd eating under white market umbrellas at two large blue picnic tables at the foot of the ramp onto the wharf. Order your meal at one window and pick it up at another; soft drinks are self-serve from a fountain machine, and thanks to the bottles on the tables, there's no skimping on vinegar and ketchup. Barb's offers burgers and vegetarian sandwiches, but the order of the day here is fish: One piece of fresh halibut, small (excellent, unpeeled) fries and cole slaw is $5.15; two pieces $9.18—not inexpensive, yet by quality a bargain. In the unlikely event that you have leftovers, you can feed the wharf gulls.

Cash only

THE BAY RESTAURANT
1701 Douglas St (385-1311)
Hours: See text

The Nonsuch Buffet, a typical department-store eatery, serves a regular Wednesday-to-Friday deal on the entree-of-the-day. For example, between the hours of 4:30 and 7:30 p.m. only, "Roast Beef Wednesday" offers the dinner plate "with all the trimmings" and coffee, tea or a soft drink for only $3.99 ($2 off the regular price); likewise, "Fish Fryday" is only $2.99. Not available at Mayfair Mall.

Credit Cards

BLUE COYOTE
1001 Wharf St (382-1969; fax: 382-1965)
Hours: Daily 8 a.m.–1 a.m.

This diner, formerly Louie Louie's, specializes in reasonably priced so-called Southwestern cuisine: Nachos (with regular and blue corn tortillas) for $5.95 and $8.95; Fire Engine Chile with homemade corn bread for $3.95 and $4.95; a 16-oz T-bone steak with mushrooms and refried beans for $15.95. But the incentives are interesting here—like half-price appetizers on Monday and Tuesday, or the occasional promotion, such as free concert tickets for every 20th meal customer. The fountain service—shakes and floats and the like—offers hard-to-find malted milk. Licensed.

Credit cards

CASA LUCINDA RESTAURANT
206 – 1483 Douglas St (383-6931)
Hours: Mon–Fri 8–8; Sat 11–9; Sun 11–5

Greek and Italian dishes highlight the menu, and there are many discount offers: An all-you-can-eat Sunday brunch ($5.95), lunch specials from $4.55 to $6.95, and dinner specials hovering around the $10 mark. The second entree is half-price if two of you are dining, and if it's a birthday and there are four in your party, a cake is complimentary.

Credit cards

CHEF ON THE RUN
2014 Oak Bay Ave (595-3151)
Hours: Mon–Fri 10–6; Sat 10–5:30

From this small deli-style store, European-trained chef Roy Greve runs a food-delivery service with a twist: It's gourmet food—like roast chicken breast with stuffing, filet mignon with Bordelaise sauce, or curried shrimp with steamed rice. Each entree comes with side dishes (potatoes, pasta, vegetables) and either soup or dessert. If you call before 2 p.m., your dinner will be delivered between 4 and 6:30 p.m. Monday to Friday only, and all of this costs a mere $5.50 per portion, tax included.

Credit cards

CHICKEN ON THE RUN
405 Craigflower Rd (385-3468)
Hours: Mon–Wed & Sun 4–9; Th–Sat 3–10

This kiosk-style joint also offers Chinese food (Szechuan and

Cantonese) under the rubric Chinese on the Way, but the real deal here is the chicken: five pieces with fries and cole slaw for $8.45; four pieces $7.35; three pieces $6.15. Though not in the league with happy-hour bar prices, the buffalo wings are $5.50 for 10. Fast delivery.

Credit cards

DEMITASSE
1320 Blanshard St (386-4442)
Hours: Mon–Fri 7–10; Sat & Sun 8–10

Before the restaurant expanded to take up most of the ground floor of the Kent Apartments/Hotel building, there was always a daunting lineup; now the place—all non-smoking—is simply packed. And no wonder—with culinary treats like the Demi Huevos, steamed-scrambled eggs with cheese, onion, salsa and green chillies in a flour tortilla ($6.25) and smoked salmon on a toasted bagel with cream cheese, onions and capers, with fresh fruit or a salad ($7.75). Hot cheese-filled croissants are a big deal here at $3.75, with additional fillings from $1 to $1.50. Desserts run along the lines of blueberry/apple or cranberry-apple pie ($3.95), Frisbee-sized oatmeal cookies ($2) and deep dark chocolate pate with raspberry sauce ($4.25). Service is brisk, but in the event of a wait, you can kill the time perusing an impressive array of local art on the walls.

Personal cheques only if they're local

FIDDLEHEADS CAFE BAKERY
1284 Gladstone Ave (386-1199)
Hours: Tue–Th 9–5; Fri & Sat 9–8

A small ground/basement-level operation opposite the Belfry Theatre specializing in an all-day breakfast ($3.95); a soup (i.e. cilantro vegetable)-and-bagel special for $3.50; and hearty, healthful sandwiches like the Fiddlehead Fave (dill cream cheese, tomato, pickle, red onion, olive and sprouts) for $3.95. Funky, fiddleheady decor.

Cash only

FOGG N' SUDS
1630 Store St (383-2337; fax: 381-7837)
Hours: Mon–Th 11–midnight; Fri 11 a.m.–1 a.m.;
Sat 10 a.m.–1 a.m.; Sun 10–11.

Newly relocated to the waterfront, this chain offers a good kids' menu ($4.95 for the likes of nachos, fish and chips, or hot dog and chips, drink included) and a hearty brunch on Saturday and Sunday from 10 a.m.–2 p.m. Seven days a week, though, the stock in trade here is an astonishing range of beers from around the world (both bottled and draught), excellent burgers starting at $5.95, pizza at $7.95 and various Mexican dishes at $8.50.

Credit cards

FOO HONG CHOP SUEY
564 Fisgard St (386-9553)
Hours: Daily (except closed Wed) 11:30–3, & 4:30–8:30;
often open later during summer evenings

Once—and still—the favourite Chinese food haunt of former B.C. Premier Dave Barrett, Foo Hong's remains a traditional Chinese food hangout for those who enjoy classic Cantonese-style cuisine. Prices are low, and as far as we can remember (back some 25 years) they've maintained a strict cash-only policy.

Cash only

HAULTAIN'S FISH & CHIPS
1127 Haultain St (383-8332)
Hours: Mon–Sat 11:30–7:30; Sun 3:30–7

Owner Mary Schmidt, who's been tending the fryers here since 1975, is too modest to say it, so we'll say it for her: This dark, comfortable, spotless shop on an otherwise residential street serves Victoria's best fish 'n' chips—the halibut ($2.75 per piece) or cod ($2.60) firm yet succulent, the batter done to crispy, golden perfection, the chips freshly cut and plentiful. Don't miss the homemade cole slaw and tartar sauce. The basket of Haultain's bookmarks, key chains and fridge magnets—free of charge, but don't abuse the privilege—is a nice, old-fashioned touch. Eat in or take out. Licensed.

Visa only

HUNTER'S
759 Yates St (384-7494)
Hours: Mon–Sat 11:30–2 a.m.; Sun 11:30 a.m.–midnight

Billing itself as a pub, grille and tapas bar, there are nibbles here for almost every taste—and cheap, too: The tapas appetizers are actually free between 4:30 and 6 on weekdays. Lunches are all $4.99. On "Mexican Mondays," wolf down as many tacos as you want for $6.99. Wednesday is "Ladies Day": 50% off dinner entrees for ladies. On Thursday, every 10th dinner is free. The mesquite-grilled steak is 99 cents per oz. Licensed.

Credit cards

ISABEL'S RIBS
1813 Douglas St (386-2722)
Hours: Mon–Sat 11:30–2:30; Mon–Th 5–9; Fri & Sat 5–10

This doesn't look much like a rib joint—more like a cafe serving European cuisine—but it does indeed live up to its claim of serving the "best ribs in town." At lunch, the house specialty is succulent beef or pork ribs with vegetables and fries or rice for $9.95. For dinner, which includes soup or salad, vegetables, and baked potato or rice, the pork spareribs, beef short ribs or beef finger ribs are $13.95 (small portion) or $16.95 (large). Licensed.

Credit cards

JOHN'S PLACE
7223 Pandora Ave (389-0711)
Hours: Mon–Th 7–10; Fri & Sat 7–11; Sun 8–3 & 5–10

JOHN'S OTHER PLACE
1652 Old Island Highway (474-6417)
Hours: Sun–Th 7–10; Fri & Sat 7–11

Excellent and inexpensive bistro-style fare is the highlight here (both places are under the same ownership). Our friend James grabs a quick lunch at the Pandora location several times a week.

The cafe atmosphere attracts a host of regulars, yet there's no sense of being an outsider if you eat alone. Great desserts, too, and a board of daily specials at modest prices.

Credit cards

KITTY CORNER CAFE
1–230 Menzies St (361-1221)
Hours: Mon 7–6; Tue–Fri 7–7; Sat 8–5:30; Sun 8–5

No wonder this neighborhood cafe in James Bay has a loyal early morning clientele: The Early Bird Breakfast Special (Mon–Fri 7–9; Sat & Sun 8–10) costs a rock-bottom $2.99 for two eggs, bacon, ham or sausage, pan fries and toast.

Cash only (or travellers' cheques)

THE MET BISTRO
1715 Government St (381-1512)
Hours: Mon–Fri from 11:30; Sat & Sun from 5

When we've wanted a really good meal fast, particularly at lunch, we've come here. It's a long, narrow, calming room, basically one long banquette punctuated by tables, with cherubs painted on the ceiling. The innovative menu items are worth an extra buck or two, although items like the oyster burger—panfried oysters, onions, Edam cheese, capers, mayo and salad—are hardly overpriced at $7.50. A recent "Festival of Pasta" promotion, from 5 p.m. onward, included the Met's Caesar salad and garlic toast. Nice wine list.

Credit cards, InterAc

OAK BAY TEA ROOM & RESTAURANT
2241 Oak Bay Ave (370-1005)
Hours: Mon–Sat 8 a.m.–9 p.m.

The early bird dinner special (Mon-Sat 4:30–6 p.m.) lets you choose one of seven two-course meals—like French lamb stew, or Beef Bourguignonne—with soup or salad, vegetables and a dinner roll, for a mere $8.95. No smoking.

Credit cards

PACIFIC RIM PIZZA
523 Pandora Ave (385-7746)
Hours: Mon–Sat 11 a.m.–3 a.m.; Sun 11 a.m.–1 a.m.

If you're window-shopping at Market Square and are feeling seriously peckish, get an immense slice-to-go here for only $3.25. Main selections include a small (12-inch) pizza with as many toppings as you like for $12.95.

Cash only

PAGLIACCI'S
1011 Broad St (386-1662)
Hours: Daily 11:30–3:30 & 5:30–11 (Fri & Sat till midnight)

This "New Yawk"-style eatery could well be the most popular restaurant in Victoria; 15 minutes after it opens for a weekday lunch, it can be full—with a lineup. (And some of the specials can seem to vanish: One day we were there early, yet the fresh lemon cream pie we had been looking forward to was sold out by 12:10 p.m.) On the menu, items can sound cute (Eggs Benedict Arnold—"a meal that won't betray you"; cheese-and-rice balls called Minnesota Fats—"Try these or we'll break your thumbs"), but the portions are seriously large (some lunch items are also available in small portions) and consistently delectable. One superb pasta: The Roman Holiday: Linguine, mushrooms, onions, bacon, egg, fontina cheese and parsley ($7.75/$6). Brisk yet friendly service in a fun, occasionally loud room festooned with appreciative-celebrity photos.

Credit cards

POUNDERS MONGOLIAN STIR FRY
535 Yates St (360-1875)
Hours: Mon–Th 11:30–10; Fri & Sat 11:30–11; Sun 4:30–10

If time, indeed, is money, then this fast, fast, *fast* food operation is a bargain by definition: You pick your own ingredients—they weigh, you pay—and then they'll prepare it in a flash. Lunch is $6.94 per pound for seafood, chicken or beef (with a 15% discount for veggie-only choices), and there's an exotic-menu dinner (including alligator, wild boar and venison) for $10.95 per pound—an extremely inexpensive way to try things you may always have wondered about.

Credit cards

THE RED MANGO/QUADRA GROCERY
1725 Quadra St (385-2827)
Hours: Mon–Fri 7:30–4:30; Sat 9–4:30; Sun noon–2; Grocery open until 5:30 Mon–Sat, Sun 10–2

The Quadra isn't so much a store—and it's certainly not a convenience store; witness the hours—as it is an anteroom for the Red Mango, an unprepossessing little cafe that serves terrific brunch and lunch fare: Monster muffins ($2.75 there; $2 to go), poached eggs on multigrain ($4.25), and various soup, salad and sandwich combos ($6.25)—all ample portions, attractively presented. Breads come from the Rising Star Bakery, while the to-die-for cinnamon raisin swirl is made on-site.

Cash only

SOPHIA'S RESTAURANT
343 Cook St (386-1455)
Hours: Tue–Fri 11:30–0; Sat & Sun 4–10

We have never been disappointed by this restaurant, which specializes in simple, moderately priced Italian dishes (lasagna $8.95, ravioli $9.50) and tasty but less inexpensive Greek ones (ie. moussaka at $13.75). But the pizzas are really what we come for; there are 30 varieties on the menu (you can build your own, of course), plus Sophia's Special: pepperoni, mushrooms, ham, green peppers, onions, black olives, shrimp, cheese and tomato sauce ($11.50 for a small).

Credit cards

TATAMI RESTAURANT
642 Johnson St (383-8892)
Hours: Daily 11:30–2:30, 4:30–10

Victoria's newest Korean/Japanese restaurant opened with an array of lunch and dinner specials worth checking out: An all-hand-rolled sushi lunch for $3.95, a Japanese seafood salad for $4.95, and, Sunday through Thursday, a two-for-one Korean barbecue dinner. Reservations necessary only for 10 or more guests.

Credit cards

VITEWAY VEGETARIAN RESTAURANT
1019 Blanshard St (384-5677; fax: 384-9533)
Hours: Mon–Fri 10–4

If you're desperate for the Big O—as in "Organic"—this is your place, tucked away in the back left side of the Viteway store: Tofu burger "with organic pickle" ($5.75), vegi chili "with organic blue corn chips" ($5.75), "fresh organic coffee" ($1). Soup of the Day, served with "Squirrelly Bread" or "Organic Brown Rice" goes for $3.55, and you can end with a tart slathered with fruit-juice-sweetened butter for $1. Note: Not open weekends, although the store is.

Credit cards

WHARFSIDE EATERY
1208 Wharf St (360-1808)
Hours: Mon–Th 11:30–11; Fri & Sat 11:30–midnight; Sun 11–10

This upscale yet casual restaurant overlooking the inner harbour always has some sort of discount promotion going. Recent specials have included prime rib for $9.95, 1 lb of crab legs for $10.95, and early bird (before 6:30) three-course dinners for $9.95.

Credit Cards

FAMILY DINING (PLACES TO TAKE CHILDREN)

FOGG N'SUDS—See General Restaurant Listings, above

FUDDRUCKER'S
787 Hillside Ave (386-4522)
Hours: Sun–Th 10–9; Fri & Sat 10–10

The best deal at this spacious, skylit, ceiling-fanned, kite-festooned joint is the 99 cent kids' special, Sundays through

Thursdays. For each adult entree, a youngster can order a small (5 oz) burger, hot dog or chicken strips, plus fries, drink and a cookie. Meanwhile, mom and dad can chow down on Fuddburgers (1/2 lb for $4.99; 1/3 lb for $4.39) or 6 oz ribeye steak sandwiches ($6.49). Beef is the big thing here, although there are also various chicken and fish dishes—any of them chased, if you like, with beer, cider or a cooler. The add-your-own-fixins area is spectacular, letting you virtually turn your burger into a salad; the soft-drink fountain is self-serve as well. Desserts, from the Goodies bar, are basically brownies ($1.89), ice cream ($.99) or pie ($2.25).

Credit cards

HARVEY'S
3253 Douglas St (475-3337)
Hours: Mon–Wed 7 a.m.–11 p.m.; Th–Sat until 3 a.m.;
Sun 8 a.m.–9 p.m.

A clean, brightly lit basic-fast-food chain operation (burgers, fries, rings) that is—not surprisingly—popular with kids (and budget-conscious parents), thanks to the "Junior Meal Deal": a burger or hot dog, fries and a soft drink for $3.27, plus a "surprise" toy.

Cash only

HUMPTY'S FAMILY RESTAURANT
811 Bay St (388-5658)
Hours: Daily 24 hrs

We were delighted to find this unpretentious, family-oriented restaurant in the strip mall at the corner of Bay and Blanshard. Staff is pleasant, and washrooms clean (always a good sign). Parents will be happy to find lots of amenities for kids: an on-going colouring contest, highchairs and bibs for tots, special children's meals and a well-situated non-smoking section. Everyone's portions are large, and desserts very fresh and tasty. A special bonus: One child can dine free (with each paying adult) from 5 to 9 pm on Fridays.

Credit cards, InterAc

THE KEG
At the Winery, 3940 Quadra St (479-1651)
At the Wharf, 500 Fort St (386-7789)
Hours: Sun–Th 4:30–10:30; Fri & Sat 4:30–11

When parents have had enough fast food with their kids and want to relax over "real" food—a nice steak, a salad bar—the Keg is the answer. Children under 12 dining with an adult eat for only $4.99 (full courses of pizza, pasta or burgers) and have unlimited access to the salad bar. A friend of ours sent her little darlings off to the salad bar right away, where they found miniature marshmallows to roast over the candle at their table on the end of a toothpick—keeping the youngsters occupied and happy while she and her husband got to enjoy a relaxing meal.

Credit cards

LEE'S FAMOUS RECIPE CHICKEN
4011 Quadra St (479-0002)
Hours: Daily 11–9

Lee's chicken really is famous, and the kids' combos can't be beat for price and value. Try the children's meal (1 piece of chicken, with fries and gravy) for $2.59 or splurge and add the roll and soft drink for just $2.79. The nugget combo is $3.39, chicken burgers start at $3.25 (alone) or $4.65 for the combo with roll, gravy, fries and soft drink. Free delivery.

Credit cards

MOXIE'S
34–3224 Saanich Rd (475-3881)
Hours: Mon–Th 10 a.m.–11 p.m.; Fri & Sat 10 a.m.–1 a.m.; Sun 9:30 a.m.–11 p.m.

If you have a hankering for chicken wings, hit this strip-mall eatery on Wednesdays after 8 p.m., when they're 25 cents each, with your choice of hot, teriyaki or honey garlic sauce. Otherwise, pick from an inexpensive 80-item menu (Philly Cheese steak, Margarita shrimp, and the like). Complete children's meals for less than $3 (plus free balloons), and selected discounts for seniors (age 55 plus). Licensed.

Credit cards

O'DONALS FAMILY RESTAURANT
1551 Cedar Hill X Rd (721-5211)
1258 Esquimalt Rd (380-6321; fax: 380-6397)
7–1516 Fairfield Rd (598-9577)
1871 Fort St (595-4442)
Hours: (All preceding locations) Daily 6 a.m.–10 p.m.

3271 Maple St (475-0111)
Hours: Daily 6 a.m.–11 p.m.

O'Donal's offers kiddies choices of chicken and chips, fish and chips, pancakes and eggs, burger or grilled cheese, each for $3.49.

Credit cards

THE PANTRY
3214 Douglas St (475-3306)
1752 Old Island Hwy (478-6212)
Hours: Daily 6:30 a.m.–11 p.m. (both)

Standard family restaurant fare and ambience with excellent bargains for kids and occasional specials for seniors. For youngsters age 10 and under, most meals are $3.75—the likes of beef macaroni and meat sauce, corn dog and fries, six silver dollar pancakes; includes a small beverage and jello or pudding. For seniors 60 and over, an entree (including juice, soup or salad) can be as low as $4.99. On Wednesday night, prices are $2.95 for kids and $4.95 for seniors.

Credit cards

PLUTO'S
1150 Cook St (385-4747)
Hours: Sun–Th 9 a.m.–11 p.m.; Fri & Sat 9 a.m.–midnight

Atmosphere—the joint is a converted gas station—and tasty mesquite-grilled cuisine make this a dandy place for breakfast or lunch, although we've found it a tad "clubby" at night, when the regulars seem to take over, the music cranks up and the overall mood changes. Piping hot and plentiful servings at good prices: A breakfast special of scrambled eggs, burrito and home-cut fries ($5.75), Sante Fe chili ($4.55), top sirloin steak burger ($7.95), vegetarian stirfry ($9.45), Mexican staples (burritos, tacos or enchiladas, with refried beans and cornsalad) for $8.95. Wonderful desserts. Licensed.

Credit cards

RED ROBIN
800 Tolmie Ave (386-4440)
Hours: Mon–Th 11–midnight; Fri & Sat 11 a.m.–1 a.m.; Sun 11–11

One of our favourite venues, combining reasonable grown-up fare with a sure-fire kids' menu—and a full range of mocktails for non-drinkers and children alike. They also have some of the most decadent desserts around. Children receive balloons and their own special menu to colour while waiting for food.

Credit cards

SMITTY'S FAMILY RESTAURANT
850 Douglas St (383-5612)
771 Vernon Ave (475-3121)
6719 West Saanich Rd (652-1764)
Hours: Daily 6:30 a.m.–11 p.m.; summers until midnight

Basically like Humpty's or The Pantry, but with an emphasis on pancakes, waffles and French toast; similarly, a good deal for children 10 and under and seniors. The kids' menu has nine items priced at $3.75 (mini pancakes and bacon, grilled cheese with fries, spaghetti with garlic toast, etc.) and four at $4.95 (grilled ham steak, sliced turkey or broiled chicken breast dinner); each includes two cookies and a beverage. Entrees on the seniors menu range in price from $3.15 to $6.15, a small Caesar salad is 99 cents, and a dessert is $1.59; as well, the regular daily special is offered at a discount.

Credit cards

SWISS CHALET CHICKEN & RIBS
3233 Douglas St (475-0334)
Hours: Daily 11 a.m.–10 p.m.

Back in the old days (read: starving college student years), we survived on the Chalet's rotisserie-cooked birds: you could get a quarter chicken dinner, including salad and beverage, for $3.25. Times—and prices—have changed, of course, and the menu has vastly expanded to include ribs and shrimp and various types of salad, but it's still a bargain: A quarter chicken dinner, with either fries or salad, though the beverage costs extra, is, 25 years later, only $5.95. Kids under 10 get the best deal of all—various chicken or rib entrees, fries or salad, milk or a soft drink, a small sundae and a grab-bag surprise for less than $4. Extremely fast and accommodating service (finger bowls, extra serviettes and condiments on request), whether you're eating there or doing takeout. Licensed.

Credit cards

UNCLE WILLY'S BUFFET
801 Vernon Ave (475-1914)
Hours: Daily 11:30–2:30 and 4–9 p.m.

When not hobnobbing with celebrities for her Vancouver *Province* "Insider" column, journalist and fashion maven Lynne McNamara likes to chow down in her favourite "real folks" eatery, Uncle Willy's. This cafeteria-style restaurant offers a vast array of self-serve, all-you-can-eat fare. It's always inexpensive, but the best deal is Sunday brunch (11:30–2:30): For $7.99 (adults), $7.39 (seniors) or 65 cents per year of age for kids (up to 11 years old), you can load up on breakfast foods (eggs, omelettes, French toast, sausages, etc.), fried chicken, roast beef, baked ham, lasagna, sundaes, cake, ice cream, coffee, tea and soft drinks. If your gang is famished, this may be the best deal in town.

Credit cards

THE WHITE SPOT
710 Caledonia St (382-9911)
3965 Quadra (727-3931)
Hours: Sun–Th 6:30 a.m.–11 p.m.; Fri & Sat until midnight

A B.C. tradition, Victoria's White Spot locations do not disappoint. The "Pirate Paks" for children under 12—macaroni and cheese ($3.45), chicken fingers ($3.75) and so on—are discounted by 50 cents if you forgo the cute cardboard packaging. Good Seniors menu: Meatloaf sandwich ($5.95), BLT ($4.45), hamburger platter ($4.25). There's an all-day breakfast (blackboard specials are a meal deal—like two eggs, two slices of bacon and two pancakes for $3.45), heart-smart specialties and, of course, the famous White Spot burger platter with "triple O" sauce and great cole slaw and fries for a mere $4.99.

Credit cards

PUBS

Victoria is an outstanding pub town—with a "local" in just about every community. In this category, we haven't deliberately overlooked some of the most famous—*The Sticky Wicket* on Douglas Street, say, or *The Elephant & Castle* in the Eaton Centre; they're certainly fine purveyors of food and drink. Rather, we've searched for pubs (a few well off the beaten tourist track) that routinely offer considerable deals on their food service, or have a particularly charming ambiance, and preferably both. Almost all pubs serve cheap beer galore and have some sort of daily-specials blackboard; we simply think that the ones described here represent the best value for your money.

THE BEAR PUB

Sidney: Hwy 17 at Beacon Ave (656-5042)

Hours: Mon–Sat 11:30 a.m.–1:30 a.m.; Sun until midnight

Not great ambiance—with its grey walls and fluorescent lighting, the place, part of the adjacent Travelodge motel, feels more like a large airport bar than a pub—but there's local beer on tap and surprisingly good grub, which you order and pick up at the Food Bar. The wings are excellent and "cheep": 25 cents apiece (15 cents on Sunday), a bucket of 50 for $12. Every night after 5 p.m. there's a daily dinner special (two-for-one on Monday, $4.95 spaghetti Thursday); on weekends until 3 p.m., steak and eggs with the works, or eggs benedict with shrimp, are $5.95.

Credit cards

ESQUIMALT INN
856 Esquimalt Rd (382-7161)
Hours: Mon 11 a.m.–12:30 a.m.; Tue–Sat until 2 a.m.; Sun noon–9

A large smoky joint with everything you'd expect from a live-music Country-&-Western joint: stage and dance floor, pool tables, jukebox and a food counter where you order from an inexpensive "Texas Grill Menu"—10 oz ribeye steak sandwich ($8.95), loaded Tacos Supremos ($4.75), Caesar salad ($3.25)—or the blackboard specials (grilled cheese sandwich and cauliflower-and-cheese soup for $4.95, hot turkey sandwich for $5.95). A mountain of Western fries is only $2.50. Ample parking.

Credit cards

5 CORNERS PUB STYLE RESTAURANT
512 Simcoe St (383-1391)
Hours: Mon–Th, Sun 11–11; Fri & Sat 11–midnight

This charming converted James Bay residence offers local (Victoria, Vancouver and Okanagan) draft for as little as $3.50 and tapas starting as low as $1.75. Excellent burgers—try the Mexican, with salsa and jalapenos, for $6.95—and an early bird three-course dinner (4–6 p.m.) for $9.95. Outdoor patio. Tough to park.

Visa only

FOUR MILE PUB
199 Island Hwy (479-3346)
Hours: Mon–Th 11:30–11:30; Fri & Sat 11:30–midnight; Sun 11:30–11

The Four Mile Roadhouse, a Victoria landmark since 1858, is now divided between an elegant restaurant and a cosy pub, the latter complete with fireplace and hanging plants, nicely furnished with replica antique captains chairs and solid oak tables. There can be great deals—wings for 25 cents, prawns for 35 cents—in addition to blackboard specials like Greek pesto chicken on penne noodles for $7.95 or a Pacific salmon melt for $6.95. The menu leans toward Tex-Mex, with a taste of the Mediterranean. Darts and TV are considerately, unobtrusively, off to one side. Downstairs, there's a cold beer and wine outlet.

Credit cards

GEORGE & DRAGON
1302 Gladstone Ave (388-4458)
4496 West Saanich Rd (479-2123)
Hours: Daily 10 a.m.–midnight (both)

We frequent the Gladstone location—a perfect spot before or after a show at the Belfry Theatre, which is kitty-corner across Fernwood. For a neighborhood pub, the food is astonishing—fresh ingredients, truly immense portions and excellent prices: At $2.95, the Dragon Fries appetizer will feed four, while, for dessert, the wonderful homemade Lemon Sour Cream Pie is a steal at $3.75. In between, there's a tantalizing array of soups, sandwiches, pasta, seafood and burgers, with a surprising nod to Indonesian cuisine. At night, the live entertainment can be enjoyed—or avoided—from any number of pleasantly mock-Tudor rooms, plus a streetside patio.

Credit cards

GORGE POINTE PUB
1075 Tillicum Road (386-5500)
Hours: Daily 11 a.m.–midnight

A brightly lit establishment too new and cavernous, even underfurnished, to be cosy—but the new menu, which specializes in Southwest and Mediterranean fare, should be a real magnet: Bayou salsa shrimp Caesar ($8.95), Sante Fe-style chicken club sandwich ($6.95) and the obligatory Gorge Pointe burger, more lavish than most: one-third lb beef, swiss and cheddar, bacon and mushrooms, green peppercorn and sun-dried tomato salsa—a deal at $7.95. Desserts are $4.95. Regular specials: a Sunday brunch burrito feast ($6.50), caffe latte on Tuesday ($2); a choice of six pastas with delicious panbread on Thursday ($7.95). Local beer on tap. Cold beer to go. Ample parking.

Credit cards, InterAc

LOGHOUSE PUB
2323 Millstream Rd (474-1989)
Hours: Mon–Th 11:30–11:30; Fri & Sat 11:30–12:30; Sun 11–midnight

Like the Gorge Pointe, too new and big to warm the cockles of your heart (built in 1988, it feels like a wanna-be lodge at Whistler), but the menu is a burger-lover's Valhalla: There are 25 versions, including the Pearl River (with melted blue cheese and bacon, $6.50) and the Neptune Chicken (with jumbo shrimp, mozzarella and cheddar, $7.50). Monday and Tuesday, wings are only 15 cents after 5 p.m., and the daily specials are well worth the money: New York steak on Sunday for $7, six tiger prawns on Wednesday for $6.50. Obligatory pool table, big-screen TV and dart boards (alas, those automated electronic ones). Patio. Ample parking.

Credit cards

MAUD HUNTER'S
3810 Shelbourne St (721-2377)
Hours: Mon–Th 11:30–midnight; Fri & Sat 11–midnight; Sun 11–11

This upstairs establishment—which CFAX's Terry Spence turned us on to—makes up for its newness with some considerable design points: there's an elevator for wheelchair patrons and easy-access, comfortable, upholstered seating. Lower than average prices for pub grub both on the menu (i.e. French onion soup for $3.95) or on the board (fish and chips for $4.95), appetizers you don't see everywhere (like two Oysters Rockefeller for $4.10), discounted draught specials on Monday and Tuesday, and a Sunday brunch for only $4.95. Darts and a small, friendly, corner stand-up bar. Cold beer and wine to go.

Credit cards

PRAIRIE INN NEIGHBORHOOD PUB
7806 East Saanich Rd (652-1575)
Hours: Mon–Th 10–midnight; Fri & Sat 11–1 a.m.; Sun 11–midnight

Established in 1893, the Prairie Inn now boasts three rooms—the most boisterous being the back sports bar, with 16 of the pub's 18 TVs—a brewery (try the Steam beer) and a well-appointed cold beer and wine "boutique." The usual appetizer board (10 tiger prawns are $4.95, a dozen wings $4.75), tempting hard-to-find sandwiches (Montreal smoked corn beef on rye with fries or salad for $5.50) and surefire desserts (carrot cake for $2). Nice, too, to see a pub cater to non-drinkers: The Prairie Inn actually promotes its coffee drinks—espresso at $1.50, cappuccino $1.75. A fun place to boot. Ample parking.

Credit cards

17-MILE PUB
5126 Sooke Rd (642-5942)
Hours: Mon–Th 11–11; Fri & Sat 11–1 a.m.; Sun 11–9

This snug (you might even say cramped) roadhouse, established in 1984 as a hunter's inn, is worth a trip out to Sooke for the food alone, which you order at the kitchen counter: garden salad with garlic bread ($3.75), fettucine Alfredo ($6.95), six oz New York steak with eggs and roast potatoes ($7.95). Large dinner appetizers start at $5.95 (wings are only 25 cents), and carnivores will delight at the 17 oz New York steak with all the trimmings for $16.95. For dessert, try the homemade cherry or pecan pie with whipped cream for $3.50. There's a small, bucolic patio and a cosy back room; despite the pool table and dart boards, this is a place for good food and conversation. Ample parking on both sides of the highway.

Visa, Travellers' cheques

SIX MILE PUB
494 Island Hwy (478-3121)
Hours: Mon–Sat 11 a.m.–1 a.m.; Sun 11 a.m.–midnight

This is a beautifully restored old pub, claiming to be the oldest in B.C. (established in 1855): four large, high-ceilinged well-lit rooms, lovely wood (check out the mahogany ceiling above the pool tables), stained glass, worn Oriental runner carpets. Eight beers on tap (some local) and standard pub fare, price- and quality-wise. Outdoor patio. Ample parking. Cold beer to go.

Credit cards

SPINNAKERS BREW PUB

308 Catherine St (386-BREW; fax: 384-3246; taproom: 384-6613)

Hours: Daily 7–10 (restaurant); 11–11 (upstairs pub)

Canada's first in-house brewpub offers a lovely view of the Inner Harbour—particularly from the upstairs balcony. Menus for breakfast, lunch and dinner run the gamut of fine pub fare, but notice the nods to the brewer's art: A highlight of the morning menu, for example, is the Brewer's Breakfast, old-fashioned hot cereal with selected malts, served with cream and toast ($4.50). The food here is excellent; for lunch, try the meal-in-itself Noggins Chowder—a creamy concoction of clams, smoked salmon, red snapper, halibut and scallops in broth—which won the 1989 Puget Sound Chowder Off (cup $3.25; bowl $4;25). And, of course, try the more than 20 beers brewed on-site, some of them available for takeout, as are the Spinnakers Brewery Breads (sourdough, Tuscan or pumpernickle for about $3, including taxes—a great deal).

Credit cards

SWANS PUB & CAFE

506 Pandora Ave (361-3310; fax: 361-3491)

Hours: Daily 11:30 a.m.–2:30 a.m. (pub), 11–11 (cafe)

With its large windows, oak beams and sandblasted brick, this is a pleasant place to sit with friends or one of the complimentary newspapers and a pint of beer, which is brewed by Buckerfield's right on the premises. If you're not sure what to sip, glasses of ale, lager, stout and bitter can be sampled for $2.75 to $2.90. The pub grub is hearty and favorably priced: Caesar salad ($5.95), a half-order of nachos, which is still ample ($5.95), Buckerfield's chili (or vegetarian chili) with beer bread ($7.95), Swans' burger with bacon, cheddar and fries ($6.95). On Fridays, get there early if you want a seat: The TGIF crowd is shoulder-to-shoulder.

Credit cards

TUDOR HOUSE PUB
533 Admirals Rd (389-9943)
Hours: Mon–Sat 11:30 a.m.–1:30 a.m.; Sun 11 a.m.–midnight

A real mishmash decor-wise—Mock Tudor with brass nautical touches, dart boards and pool tables at one end, sunken-dance-floor disco and giant TV at the other—but solid pick-up food and cheap beer: a glass of draft is $2, a mug $3.60; the burgers start at $4.95, a small poutine is $4.45, and three-piece fish and chips run $6.95. Ample parking.

Credit cards

THE WADDLING DOG INN
2476 Mt. Newton X Rd (652-1146; fax: 652-4946; wine & beer store 652-1723)
Hours: Daily 11 a.m.–1 a.m. (pub); 9 a.m–11 p.m. (beer store)

If it's Sunday afternoon, and you have the munchies, this is the place to go: After 4 p.m., the entire pub menu—excluding the daily specials—is 50 per cent off. Even the normal prices for the hearty fare are good: Nachos for two ($8.95), three-decker clubhouse ($5.95), clam chowder ($3.95) and the humungous Waddling Dog burger (two patties and a split hot dog, with fries or Caesar salad, $5.95). As for the daily specials, sandwiches start as low as $1.99. Ample parking. Cold beer and wine to go next door.

Credit cards

NOTES:

2. RECREATION & HOBBIES

ENTERTAINMENT: FILMS, PERFORMING ARTS, REPERTORY THEATRES

BOX OFFICE TICKET SALES
2950 Douglas St (388-9863, 475-3077; fax: 475-3466)
Hours: Mon–Fri 9–5:30; Sat 8:30–4

This is the ticket sales outlet for Deborah J. Cameron's Imagery Beyond Performing Arts Society, which produces local concerts and other performing arts events—everything from opera to rock. Tickets for all of Imagery Beyond's events are available here—sans surcharge—as is info on upcoming productions.

Cheques, MasterCard only

ERIC MARTIN THEATRE
2334 Trent St (see text)
Hours: Mon—See text

Everyone is welcome to watch videos on the big screen every Monday (starting at about 7 p.m.) at the Eric Martin Theatre, located right across from Shoppers Drug Mart and near the south entrance to the Royal Jubilee's Eric Martin Pavilion Building at Trent and Fort St. Admission is free. Popcorn (with real butter, no less) and pop are available cheaply. Movies shown are usually recent releases. For details on what's playing, call the Royal Jubilee switchboard at 595-9200.

Free; pay cash for treats

GREAT CANADIAN CASINO
3075 Douglas St (380-3998; fax: 380-7345)
3366 Douglas St (475-2614)
Hours: Daily 6 p.m.–2 a.m.

Legal casino gambling is great entertainment. There's no admission charge (most people risk $25–$50 for an evening's fun), but alcohol is prohibited. Call for details on their free gaming lessons (between 6 and 7 p.m. weekdays). Says marketing honcho Cary Corbeil, "We want you to win, because then you'll tell your friends and you'll all come back." Try your hand at roulette, blackjack, red dog or their innovative Sic Bo wheels. And don't take more than you can afford to lose.

Cash only

THE ROXY THEATRE
2657 Quadra St (382-3370)
Hours: See text

Victoria's oldest repertory theatre offers student discounts (about 30% off—show your ID), comfy seats (including padded bench seats in the back rows), and off-beat films. Old ceiling fans cool the auditorium, which is shaped like a quonset hut, and every seat has its own drink holder attached to the row in front. If you attend during one of its film festivals, there's a $1 one-time-only surcharge for "membership". Film times are generally 7:15 and 9:15 p.m. and "midnight" shows usually start about 11:15 Friday and Saturday evenings. The box office opens just shortly before show time at around 6:45.

Cash only

AUDIO & VIDEO EQUIPMENT

ATLAS STEREO & TV

821 Fort St (385-2712)

Hours: Mon–Sat 9–5:30

Specializes in Hitachi, Panasonic and JVC lines, with a standard 13-month payment schedule. VCRs start at $30 per payment, 20-inch TVs at $40, 27-inch TVs at $79. Atlas also has a good selection of used electronics.

Credit cards

BC SOUND & RADIO

1805 Fort St (595-4225)

Hours: Mon–Fri 8:30–5:30; Sun 10–2

This shop provides VCR cleaning and repairs from just $29.95, and all work is guaranteed.

Cheques, Credit cards

CIRCUIT CITY

488C Bay St (383-9877)

Hours: Mon–Wed & Sat 10–6; Th & Fri 10–9; Sun noon–5

Stocks major brands of audio equipment, TVs and VCRs (Sanyo, RCA, Toshiba, Zenith, Kenwood, Harman Kardon) and has occasional warehouse clearance sales. Recent deals: 26-inch Sanyo monitor-style TV for $399; Zenith four-head VCR with VCR Plus for $288; Kenwood AM/FM theft-proof auto cassette deck for $179. Some sale items may be demonstration models.

Credit cards

FUTURE SHOP

2950 Douglas St (386-5661)

Hours: Mon–Fri 10–9; Sat 10–6; Sun 11–5

This chain has broadened its inventory far beyond electronics to include computers (of course) but also washer/dryers, fridges, stoves and freezers, microwaves, camcorders, fax machines and more. But it has been—rightly, we think—criticized for its aggressive sales staff and indifferent returns/repair stance. Still, its loss leaders are usually great buys (if you can resist the up-sell to a more expensive model), and Future Shop's seasonal sales are legendary.

Credit cards, InterAc

MAIS RENT-TO-OWN
485 Burnside (385-2435; fax: 385-1267
Hours: Mon–Sat 9:30–5:30; Sun 11–4

CanWest Mall, 2945 Jacklin Rd (474-5355)
Hours: Mon–Th & Sat 9–5:30; Fri 9–9; Sun 11–4

This company has been serving Victoria since the 1940s, offering sales, rentals and service on electronic equipment (TVs, stereos, VCRs, camcorders), furniture and appliances (microwaves, dishwashers, fridges, washers, dryers, ranges). They also take trade-ins and sell rental returns outright at discount prices. Free local delivery.

Credit cards

MULTITECH WAREHOUSE
3080 Blanshard St (386-6002)
Hours: Mon–Fri 10–9; Sat 9–6; Sun 11–5

Another caveat-emptor place, thanks to commissioned salespeople who might try to up-sell you once you're in the store. Still, we've found incredible deals—especially on loss leaders—among the everyday great buys in TVs, stereo components, car stereos, microwaves, camcorders, computers and electronic keyboards. Remember to stick to what you came for (in other words, don't get talked into a lot of accessories you might not need), and do some comparison shopping before buying.

Cheques, Credit cards

PAMUS MUSIC
1108 Blanshard St (386-8475)
Hours: Tue–Sat 9:30–5:30

Among local musicians, Pamus has an excellent reputation for their fair dealing in musical instruments, expert advice before you buy, and support afterward. They buy, sell and trade second-hand instruments and accessories.

Credit cards

SOUND HOUNDS
1532 Pandora St (595-4434; service dept: 598-8613)
Hours: Mon–Sat 9:30–6

According to our friend James, the sales staff here really know their stuff and won't try to hype you into buying something inappropriate to your needs. Excellent after-sale service.

Cheques, Credit cards, InterAc

UNIVERSAL TRADING CENTRE PAWNBROKERS
584 Johnson St (383-9512)
Hours: Mon–Sat 9–5:30; Sun 10–5

A classic pawnshop that buys, sells and trades in jewellery, cameras, stereos, TVs, sporting goods, guns, motorcycles, general household goods and even cars and boats. They accept pawned goods on a 30-day renewable contract, and you reclaim your items by full interest payment.

Cash preferred

VIDEO ONLY
749 Pandora St (381-7733)
Hours: Mon–Wed & Sat 9–6; Th & Fri 9–9; Sun 11–5

This "Discount Specialty Store" is similar to Future Shop and Multitech: everyday low prices on brand name (RCA, Hitachi, Goldstar, Mitsubishi, Pioneer, Sony) TVs and VCRs and camcorders. Offers six-month interest-free financing for $1 down on a purchase.

Cheques, Credit cards

AUDIO & VIDEO RECORDINGS, CDS, VIDEO GAMES & RENTALS

A & B SOUND
641 Yates St (385-1461)
Hours: Mon–Wed 9–6; Th & Fri 9–9; Sat 9–6; Sun 11–5

A vast, reasonably priced selection of TVs, VCRs, microwaves, home and car stereo systems, phones and answering machines, cassettes and decks, CDs and players. Given its chain-wide buying power, A&B's prices on CDs and pre-recorded tapes are virtually unbeatable, and there's almost always something on sale in every category. Virtually every one of our insiders recommended A&B, and several made reference to their super periodic sales on CDs and cassettes.

Cheques, Credit cards

BOOMTOWN
711 Yates St (380-5090; fax: 380-0121)
Hours: Mon–Wed 10–6; Th–Fri 10–9; Sat 10–6; Sun noon–6

A compact disc rental operation with special rates for members: For example, two CDs for two nights will cost a member $2 and a non-member $3.25. (A trial three-month membership costs $20 plus tax and includes two free rentals). Returns are due by 4 p.m., but the overdue charge is reasonable: $1 per day per disc. A deposit is required on bulk rentals. Boomtown also sells used CDs at a discount.

Credit cards

CHOICE MUSIC
University Heights, 3980 Shelbourne St (472-0583)
Hours: Mon–Th & Sat 9:30–5:30; Fri 9:30–9; Sun noon–5

Bills itself as "Victoria's only listen-before-you-buy CD & tape store." (The idea is that you can preview your purchases and avoid disappointment.) There's also a free membership in their Choice Music Club.

Cheques, Credit cards

DOUG'S VIDEO GAMES
1014 Cook St (383-6083)
Hours: Mon–Fri 9–8; Sat 9–5:30; Sun noon–2

Offering Vancouver Island's largest selection of video games, Doug's buys, sells and trades Nintendo, Genesis, Gameboy, Gamegear, Super Nintendo and CD games of every kind. A modest discount is given to seniors. Easy wheelchair access.

Credit cards, InterAc

ENDANGERED SPECIES
890 Fort St (360-0098)
Hours: Mon–Sat 10–5:30

Specializes in jazz and blues (tapes, CDs and books); buys, sells and trades tapes and videos (new & used); good prices on blank tapes.

Credit cards

HOMETECH ELECTRONICS
Burnside Plaza, 3460 Tillicum Rd (361-1881)
Hours: Mon–Th & Sat 10–6; Fri 10–7:30; Sun 11–5

Genesis, Nintendo, Super Nintendo, Game Boy, Game Gear and CD ROM are bought, sold and traded here, seven days a week.

Cheques, Credit cards

LYLE'S PLACE
726 Yates St (382-8422; fax: 382-4542)
Langford: 711 Goldstream Ave (478-9272)
Hours: Mon–Th & Sat 10–5:30; Fri 10–9; Sun noon–5 (both)

Trade your used CDs, cassettes and videos for cash; buy two used videos and get one free. There's always a table of sale-priced CDs, and a selection of movie posters and T-shirts. Lyle's also buys CDs, cassettes, videos and laser discs. Easy handicapped access.

Credit cards

MEZZROW'S MUSIC & BOOKS
Town & Country, 19 – 3571 Douglas St (475-2633)
Hours: Mon–Th & Sat 10–5:30; Fri 10–8; Sun 12:30–4:30

One of the last bastions of the good ol' LP record, which routinely sell for 50% off at Mezzrow's. Regular specials on used cassettes, collectors' comic books and paperbacks.

Credit cards

THAT'S ENTERTAINMENT!
903 Yates St (383-0111)
Hours: Mon–Th 9–11; Fri & Sat 9–midnight; Sun 10–11

A convenient clearinghouse for used videos and video games—buy, sell or trade. "Previously viewed" movies, of which That's Entertainment! literally stocks thousands, can be had for as little as $1.88. As for new product, a recent deal on the Sega/Genesis system cost $119.99 after the manufacturer's rebate.

Credit cards

TILLICUM AUDIO VIDEO
1008 Tillicum Rd (383-5449)
Hours: Mon–Sat 9–7; Sun noon–6

They buy, sell and trade CDs, video games (Genesis, Super Nintendo, Game Gear, CD ROM, etc.) and also provide repairs on CD players, stereos and Nintendo machines.

Cheques, Credit cards

THE TURNTABLE
107 – 3 Fan Tan Alley (382-5543)
Hours: Mon–Th & Sun 10–5:30; Fri 10–7; Sat 10–6

Quality used tapes, CDs and LPs are bought, sold and traded here. The emphasis is on folk (domestic and international), and the atmosphere is funky.

Credit cards

BOOKS, MAPS, COLLECTIBLE CARDS & COMICS

AAAABA BOOK CITY
1600 Quadra St (389-0777)
Hours: Mon–Sat 10–5, closed Wed; Sun noon–5

We suppose owner Lloyd Cartwright was determined to be first in the phone book (believe it or not, he's second in the Victoria book), but he's still first in ours. His well-trained dalmation, Sir Duke, is always there among the old movie posters, magazines, books, calendars, newspapers, tapes, records and sheet music in the cavernous 1912 landmark building, which was once a Baptist church. If you're looking for a calendar for the year of your sweetie's birth, here's the place—and Lloyd can find it for you. And if you have a credit carried over from the days when AAAABA was in Vancouver, he'll honour it in Victoria. Choose a free book from a special bin with every purchase and look for the special 50%-off sections throughout the store. Even the building is for sale—make an offer (asking price is $995,000).

Cheques, Credit cards

AVALON METAPHYSICAL CENTRE—**See Occult, Metaphysical & Wiccan**

BEACON BOOKS & COLLECTABLES
Sidney: 9807 3rd St (655-4447)
Hours: Mon–Sat 9–5:30; Sun noon–4

Always a good browse, this smallish, used bookstore also sells stamps, coins and music books.

Cheques, Credit cards

BOLEN BOOKS
Hillside Centre, 78 – 1644 Hillside Ave (595-4232; fax: 595-1458)
Hours: Mon, Tue & Sat 9:30–5:30; Wed–Fri 9:30–9; Sun 11–5

Recommended by our friends Marilyn and Cary, this large book-seller carries a good selection of alternative health and healing books. Emphasis is also on computer and business titles. There's also a table of remainders at clear-out prices.

Credit cards

BOOK ENDS PUBLISHERS CLEARANCE OUTLET
907 Yates St (380-0740)
Hours: Mon–Fri 10–6; Sat 10–5; Sun noon–5

This discount bookstore offers an ever-changing, and therefore unpredictable, inventory, averaging 50% off the cover price. It's not a good place if you're searching for a specific title, but it is if you're just looking for a good book in a specific category (say, a nice cookbook for a birthday present). The last time we dropped by, the categories (alphabetically) included art, biography, business, computers, cooking, crafts and decorating, fiction, health, kids, sports and travel.

Credit cards

BOOK WAREHOUSE
1301 Government St (386-5711)
Hours: Daily 10–10

This is the only Victoria outlet of a successful lower mainland chain that deals primarily in remainder and bankruptcy stock, offering discounts of 50% (and sometimes as much as 90%) in such areas as gardening, travel, home improvement, art, history, psychology, health, crafts, cooking, the occult, children's interests, home decor and repair, reference books and Canadiana. There are lesser—but still substantial—discounts on computer books and current hardcover best sellers. Schools get an extra 10% off for orders over $100. The best bargain is the coffee: It's free.

Cheques, credit cards

BOOKS & CRANNIES
145 Menzies St (385-4519)
Hours: Mon–Th, Sat & Sun 10–5; Fri 10–9

This cosy little James Bay bookshop buys, sells and trades used books. Good browsing.

Cheques

COASTAL COOKBOOK CO
114–2187 Oak Bay Ave (595-5208)
Hours: Mon–Sat 9:30–5:30

All they stock is cookbooks—but what a selection. Occasional deals on discontinued items. Free mailing service (order by phone).

Cheques, Credit cards

CONTRAILS—THE AVIATOR STORE
19 Bastion Sq (361-4745)
Hours: Mon–Fri 9:30–5:30; Sat 10–5; Sun noon–4

This specialty store is the only place in town to buy books, videos and calendars for the aviator in your life. They also stock pins, patches, caps, prints, posters, cards and flight accessories.

Credit cards

CROWN PUBLICATIONS
521 Fort St (386-4636; fax: 386-0221)
Hours: Mon–Fri 8:30–5; Sat 9:30–5

Seldom a bargain, but often the only place to buy official books. Here's where to get all manner of government publications, including nautical charts and topographical maps. Recently relocated (June/94) from Yates St. Easy wheelchair access.

Credit cards

CURIOUS COMICS & CARDS
625 Johnson St (384-1656; fax: 384-7140)
Burnside Plaza, 3478 Tillicum Rd (383-8264)
Hours: Mon–Sat 10–6; Sun 10:30–4:30

This is Victoria's headquarters for comic books, collectible trading cards (sport and non-sport), role-playing games, T-shirts and posters.

Victoria-area cheques, Credit cards

EARTH QUEST BOOKS
1286 Broad St (361-4533)
Hours: Mon–Th & Sat 10–5:30; Fri 10–6

This travel bookstore offers the city's best assortment of maps, guidebooks and travel literature.

Cheques, Credit cards

FAIRFIELD BOOK SHOP
Cook St Village, 247 Cook St (386-9095)
Hours: Mon–Sat 10–5; Sun noon–5

Buy, sell and trade new and used books. They also have a selection of new remaindered books at good discounts.

Cheques, Credit cards

THE FIELD MATURALIST (natural history books)—**See Recreation & Hobbies**

GOODWILL STORE (gigantic book sale)—**See Charity Resale & Thrift Stores**

THE HAUNTED BOOKSTORE
Market Square, 13–560 Johnson St (382-1427)
Hours: Mon–Sat 10–5; Sun noon–5

Funky grey stone walls provide the backdrop for reading areas, framed art of literary heroes—and great book browsing. Marina Gerwing's shop is what we'd call a "serious" used bookstore.

Credit cards

HAWTHORNE BOOKSHOP
1027 Cook St (383-3215)
Hours: Mon–Sat 10–5:30

A wide selection of new and used books, particularly those concerning the arts and humanities. They'll also mail-order worldwide and offer free search for out-of-print books.

Cheques, Credit cards

IVY'S BOOKSHOP
2184 Oak Bay Ave (598-2713; fax: 595-1552)
Hours: Mon–Th & Sat 9:30–6; Fri 9:30–9; Sun noon–4

Here's a charming browse-around bookstore. Amid the carefully selected full-price stock is a small selection of remainders and discontinued books at discounted prices. Relocated earlier this year to larger premises on Oak Bay Ave.

Cheques, Credit cards

LAWRENCE EDDY BOOKS—See Office Needs

LONDON DRUGS (book bargains; computer books)—See Photography

MUNRO'S BOOKS
1108 Government St (382-2464)
Hours: Mon–Wed & Sat 9–6; Th & Fri 9–9; Sun 11–5

Because Munro's carries some 60,000 titles at any given time, its sales tables, despite the staff's attentiveness to inventory return, are always interesting. Relatively recent hardcovers can be as much as 60 per cent off, and there are often great deals on coffee-table tomes. However, the sale-book area is also smack in the centre of the store, so good luck getting out without buying something new, too. Prompt special-order service.

Cheques, Credit cards

MILITARY BOOK HOUSE
Royal Mall, 731C Fort St (384-2346; fax: 534-4166)
Hours: Mon–Sat 10–5:30

Chuck Bainbridge has the only bookstore in Victoria specializing in military books, maps and prints. He'll also provide appraisals of your military items.

Cheques, Credit cards

SMART BOOK SHOP
Shelbourne Plaza, 3643 Shelbourne Ave (721-4200)
Hours: Mon–Sat 9:30–6; Sun noon–5

New and used books are bought, sold and traded here. Among the choices: Pocket books, children's, Canadiana, reference, literature, history, comics and publishers' remainders.

Credit cards

SMITHBOOKS

CanWest Shopping Centre, 124–Jacklin Rd (478-3543)
Mayfair Shopping Centre, 547–3147 Douglas St (381-2700)
Tillicum Mall, 19–3170 Tillicum Rd (381-3034)
Town & Country, 10–3599 Douglas St (475-2488)
2 Victoria Eaton Centre (385-3077)
Hours: Mall hours, generally Mon–Wed & Sat 9:30–5:30; Th & Fri 9:30–9; Sun noon–5

Each location—but particularly Town and Country (which we favour for easiest parking)—carries a large stock of remainders, often at 50% off the last marked price. Reductions can be as much as 90% off original suggested retail. At the Town and Country store, fully half of the shelf space is dedicated to remainders. Smiths also offer something called The Paperback Club: Buy five books, get one book free (some restrictions apply, inquire at branch). We've also found 50% discounts on display tables near the front window on pens, stationery, potpourri and miscellany. Also ask about the Smitty Book Club (for kids).

Credit cards

SRI ATMANS METAPHYSICAL BOOKSTORE—**See Occult & Metaphysical**

TANNERS—A BOOKSTORE & MORE

Sidney: 2436 Beacon Ave (656-2345; fax: 656-0662)
Hours: Daily 8 a.m.–10 p.m. (summer); 8–9 (winter)

Great browsing, a good children's section and a discount table (hardcovers up to 50% off) draw us back repeatedly to Tanners. In fact, if we know we're going to miss the next ferry, we'll almost always detour into Sidney for a prolonged visit. The map room at the back has a sale table of travel books, not too outdated, for up to 40% off. Tanner's offers mail order service everywhere, and special orders are filled promptly.

Credit cards

TRIPLE SPIRAL BOOKS & BLACK MADONNA—See Occult & Metaphysical

YM-YWCA BOOK SALE—See 11A, Community Sales

YATES NEWS & BOOKS
736 Yates St (383-6634)
Hours: Mon–Fri 7:30–7; Sat 9–7

It's not much of a bookstore—it's fine if you're looking for the latest Ludlum, Steel or Krantz—and it's an OK newsstand (leaning, in terms of out-of-town newspapers, toward the Brit tabloids), but it's definitely a *world-class* magazine rack. We've found magazines here we couldn't find at Mayfair News in Vancouver, Lichtman's in Toronto or Book Soup in Los Angeles. Other than the occasional book sale, there are no deals here. But if you're homesick or lost or merely curious, its periodicals and hard-to-find maps are well worth paying full retail. Frustratingly, it's not open on our favorite browsing day: Sunday.

Credit cards (only on $10 or more)

WIMSEY BOOKS
Market Square, 110–560 Johnson St (380-1764)
Hours: Mon–Sat 10–5; Sun noon–4

Mysteries, thrillers and true crime books. Like the clues in a good murder mystery, this store is small, easy to miss and immensely rewarding upon discovery. There's a good range of new hardcovers and paperbacks, but the attractions are the used books and the exceptionally informed and tenacious staff, who will, like the detective, track down what you want.

Credit cards

OCCULT, METAPHYSICAL & WICCAN SUPPLIES

AVALON METAPHYSICAL BOOKS
62–560 Johnson St (380-1721; same for fax)
Hours: Mon–Sat 10–6; Sun noon–6

Gifts, masks, crystals, runestones, shamanic items, body oils and a huge stock of books make Avalon the first place to go for occult and healing supplies. The ad for a recent sale here said "You don't have to be psychic to know these are great deals!"—and savings were indeed self-evident: 20–70% off on such stock as goddess statues, tarot cards, magical jewellery and books. There was even a quartz crystal skull (one only) valued at $1,000 on sale for $449. Sales tend to be timed for equinox periods or other symbolic times. This is a serious endeavour—most of the clientele being "practitioners". Many thanks to Masha for all her help and advice, by the way.

Credit cards

BUZZARD'S LUNCH
536 Herald St (380-7284)
Hours: Closed Mon; Sun & Tue noon–5; Wed & Th noon–7; Fri & Sat noon–10

Buzzard's Lunch (charming name) functions mainly as an art gallery—exploring the mystic and profane, of course—but they also stock some lovely pieces of Celtic jewellery and wiccan trappings, at very reasonable prices.

Cheques

INSTINCT ART & GIFTS
622 View St (388-5033)
Hours: Mon–Sat 10:30–5:30; Sun noon–5

More upmarket than spooky, this place sells gifts and novelties, dragons, Tibetan singing bowls, drums, rain sticks, wind chimes, massage oils, plus some serious metaphysical stuff.

Cheques, Credit cards

SRI ATMANS METAPHYSICAL BOOKSTORE
1308 Government St (383-3032)
Hours: Mon–Sat 10–5:30

A full range of metaphysical and what we might loosely call "alternative lifestyle" tomes and supplies, plus expert advice on meditation and transformation.

Cheques, Credit cards

TRIPLE SPIRAL BOOKS & BLACK MADONNA
106 – 3 Fan Tan Alley (380-7212)
Hours: Mon–Sat noon–5

Ariel and Jessica provide metaphysical supplies, dream interpretation, tarot decks, palmistry, runes, numerology and astrology paraphernalia, and advice appropriate to working in the mystic arts.

Cheques

PERFECT SCENTS (incense)—See Cosmetics

SILK ROAD (body elixirs, essential oils)—See Cosmetics

PHOTOGRAPHIC SUPPLIES

KERRISDALE CAMERAS
841 Vernon Ave (475-2066)
Hours: Mon–Sat 9–5:30

Our bargain maven Marilyn Wargo likes Kerrisdale for its policy of taking trade-ins toward a new purchase, which is a real price-break. This family-run business since 1961 claims to have the largest selection of new and used photo equipment in Western Canada. Good after-sale service.

Cheques, Credit cards, InterAc

LENS & SHUTTER CAMERAS
615 Fort St (383-7443)
Hours: Mon–Sat 9:30–5:30

Lens & Shutter promised to match any local competitor's price for camera equipment—even if you find the same item on sale within 30 days of your purchase at L&S. Sale prices on regular goods are very competitive, and their own line of accessories is high-quality and low-priced. They provide rentals, take trade-ins and sell used equipment at bargain prices.

Cheques, Credit cards, InterAc

LONDON DRUGS CAMERAS
127 – 3995 Quadra St (727-3324)
201 – 911 Yates St (381-1454)
1907 Sooke Rd (474-6557)
Hours: Mon–Sat 9 a.m.–10 p.m.; Sun 10–8 (all)

We had to include London Drugs because of its fantastic deals on cameras, camera equipment and accessories. Its flyers go out province-wide twice a month, and every one features a host of camera items at prices that are often below dealer cost. If the item you're after is not sale-priced right now, chances are it will be soon. Sales staff are very helpful at tipping you off if something they carry is about to go on sale. Lots of deals on one-hour photofinishing. A superior selection of computer how-to books. Our thanks to supervisor Carmen for helping when we sought a special item.

Cheques, Credit cards

BIKES & CYCLING SUPPLIES, RENTALS & REPAIRS

A-1 BICYCLES, MODELS & SCOOTER RENTALS
727 Courtney St (386-5122)
Hours: Daily 8–6:30

This is the bike rental shop that serves the downtown core—and where all those smiling tourists on their putt-putting scooters found 'em. Prices are reasonable for short-term rentals.

Cheques, Credit cards

CAP'S BICYCLES
1942 Blanshard St (360-1999)
Hours: Mon, Tue & Sat 10–6; Wed–Fri 10–9; Sun 11–5

Though the original Cap's was established in 1932, this version is a self-proclaimed "warehouse store." The deal everyone waits for is "the Big One"—the annual week-long sale with savings up to 60% on literally thousands of top-name bikes, accessories, helmets and equipment. All kinds of other money-saving options are offered year-round, including split-payment plans, discount coupons with bike purchase, and their "service solution" two-year labour warranty plan.

Credit cards, InterAc, financing plan

CARL'S MOUNTAIN & CITY BICYCLES
Oak Bay: 1967 Oak Bay Ave (598-2453)
Gordon Head: 3705 Stamboul St (721-2453)
Hours: Mon–Fri 9–6; Sat 9–5; Sun 11–4

Top name brands are highlighted here, plus cycle cross-training clothing, expert advice and everything for the serious cycle enthusiast. Carl's also organizes the annual Mud Mosh mountain bike race. Student discounts.

Credit cards, InterAc

THE CYCLEPATH
1025 Fort St (384-6665)
450 Burnside Rd E (383-1331)
Hours: Mon–Fri 10–6; Sat 10–5; Sun noon–5 (both)

It claims to be "the biggest bike chain around," which explains its buying power and why its prices are so competitive. Guarantees are "hassle free," and bike assembly is free. Periodic sales offer savings from 25–40% off regular prices.

Cheques, Credit cards

FAIRFIELD BICYCLE SHOP
1275 Oskar St (381-2453)
Hours: Mon–Fri 9–6; Sat 9–5; Sun 11–4

This is actually our neighbourhood bicycle shop, but we were tipped to it by friends Jan and James, who describe it as "small, personable, family-oriented and very good."

Cheques, Credit cards

MAC'S CYCLE CENTRE
3627 Shelbourne St (477-7612)
Hours: Mon–Th & Sat 9:30–5:30; Sun 11–3

The focus is on parts and accessories, sales and service. They offer student discounts, too.

Cheques, Credit cards

OAK BAY BICYCLE
1968 Oak Bay Ave (598-4111; fax: 598-9477)
Hours: Mon–Th 9–5;30; Fri 9–7; Sat 9–5

This small store has an amazingly resourceful inventory—something for every level of expertise and lifestyle. Owner Louis Barnard performs quick and reasonable repairs (the company has been established in Victoria more than 60 years). Related to Sidney Cycles, 9711 Fifth St (655-1555).

Credit cards

PACIFIC CYCLE
721 Yates St (380-7060)
Hours: Mon–Th 9:30–6:30; Fri 9–9; Sat 9:30–6; Sun 11–5

This large store offers consignment rates, selection, service and accessories. They carry a huge inventory of bikes, helmets and clothing to fit every price range.

Cheques, Credit cards

RENO BIKES
2519-2521 Government St (384-5514)
Hours: Mon–Sat 9–5:30; Sun noon–5

All major brands are available on a buy-sell-trade basis (new and used). There are loads of accessories, bike shorts, safety gear and everything from the revolutionary design of the Allsop racing bikes (for $2,900), right down to kiddie trikes. (The showroom is so large, they must post a sign to warn: "no riding inside, please.") Reno promises "lowest prices guaranteed" and offers budget-plan financing. Easy wheelchair access.

Cheques, Credit cards, Telecheck, financing

RIDER'S CYCLES
1092 Cloverdale Ave (381-1125; fax: 386-0408)
Hours: Mon–Th & Sat 9–6; Fri 9–9; Sun 11–4

There's a large selection of parts, clothing and accessories here and perks like a free water bottle and cage with certain purchases. Bikes come with a one-year full service and warranty pledge. Watch for periodic clearout sales with savings of 25–40% off.

Credit cards

RUSS HAY'S BICYCLE SHOP
650 Hillside Ave (384-4722; fax: 384-8860)
Hours: Mon–Th & Sat 9–5:30; Fri 9–9
Sidney: 2480 Beacon Ave (656-1512)
Hours: Mon–Sat 9–5:30

Sometimes known simply as "The Bicycle Shop," these stores have been serving the Victoria community since 1959 with what they term "the largest selection of bicycles, accessories, parts, clothing and home fitness equipment on the Island." They often advertise substantial discounts on top-line bikes, like the Nishiki Colorado at $259.99 recently (it's regularly $319.99).

Cheques, Credit cards, InterAc

SPORT MART—**See Sporting Goods & Recreational Clothing**

SPORTS TRADERS—**See Sporting Goods & Recreational Clothing**

SPORTING GOODS & RECREATIONAL CLOTHING

THE BOATERS EXCHANGE
Sidney: 10221 McDonald Pk (655-3101; fax: 655-4399)
Hours: Mon–Sat 9:30–5

This marine surplus store looks as nautical as it is bargain-conscious. They sell everything from coloured floats to signal flares to floatation vests, at prices for new goods that you'd expect to pay for used. They carry typical surplus items, too.

Credit cards

CAPITAL IRON (sporting goods)—**See Building Materials**

CLUBS 4 YOU
1719 Quadra St (385-4653; 1-800-665-0077)
Hours: Mon–Fri 10–5:30; Sat 10–4

Highly regarded by two of the most serious golfers we know in Victoria (yes, Bob, you're one of them), this place continues to be a good source for discount clubs, replacement shafts and all sorts of golfing paraphernalia. All major manufacturers are represented in their stock, and they offer a lifetime warranty on all irons—presuming you don't do a Jack Nicholson with one and go after someone's car.

Cheques, Credit cards

COASTLINE SURF AND SPORT
152–560 Johnson St (382-2123; fax: 383-8047)
Hours: Mon–Fri 10–6; Sat 10–5; Sun noon–5

Here we found surfing gear, warm jackets and deep discounts for clearance items (50–60% off), plus those wonderful Stussy shirts from the U.S. at competitive prices.

Credit cards

COOK DESIGN STUDIOS (team sportswear)—**See Factory Outlets**

CROWN PUBLICATIONS (nautical charts)—**See Books**

DISCOUNT FIREWORKS
Milnes Landing Store, 6250 Sooke Rd (642-3115)
Otter Point Grocery, 7871 West Coast Rd (642-3211)
Hours: See text

These are two locations that pop up every fall (until Hallowe'en) to sell Burning Schoolhouses, Screechers, Volcanoes, assorted fountains, Roman candles and other traditional fireworks, all at prices 30–50% off regular retail. Assortments are well-chosen for extra family value, and we've found they offer good advice about choosing and handling fireworks, without pressure sales tactics or up-selling. Hours are generally 9:30 to 6, with extended hours toward the end of October, so you can shop after work or school.

Cash only

FACTORY TACKLE SALES
Sidney: 9756A 3rd St (656-1459; fax: 656-3988)
Hours: Mon–Fri 9:30–4:30; Sat 10–4:30

Manufacturing fishing tackle since 1972, this factory direct shop now promises "good ol' fishin' prices" at its original location, also known as O'Ki Tackle Manufacturing. Follow signs around to the side of the factory to find the outlet shop's door. Owner Brian Smith pledges: "We can give the best deals on fishing tackle, period." They stock a full inventory of lines and can put together gift packages for your favourite fisherman at almost any budget.

Credit cards

FAWCETT SHOE REPAIR (renew runners)—See Shoes & Footwear

THE FIELD NATURALIST
1241 Broad St (388-4174)
Hours: Mon–Sat 9:30–5:30

Victoria's telescope specialists offer periodic sales and can repair most models.

Credit cards

FIREWORKS CITY (Sept. and Oct only)
2510 Douglas St
2041 Oak Bay Ave
70 Gorge Rd
676 Granderson
Sidney: 10426 Resthaven Rd
Hours: See text

Like Discount Fireworks, these outlets appear like mushrooms after the rain—well, actually, after Labour Day—and offer a huge selection and lowest prices on most domestic-use fireworks. Some examples from last year: Roman candles, 5-ball at 59 cents and 12-ball for $1.10; Hummeroos for $3.49 and the best-selling Air Bombs (watch out!) for $1.95. Hours are generally 9:30 to 6 weekdays, with extended hours as Hallowe'en approaches. They absorb the GST and PST into their quoted prices.

Cash only

FRANK WHITE'S SCUBA SHOP
1855 Blanshard St (385-4713)
Sidney: 2537 Beacon Ave (656-9202)
Hours: Daily 9–5:30 (both)

If you've always wanted to dive (we do) but are daunted by the cost (we are), consider Frank White's if and when the time comes to buy your equipment. Friends who've bought here say the sale prices have been hard to beat: 3mm Neoprene shorty suits for $69.95 (regularly $140), used 6mm wet suits for $99, and used regulators and gauges starting at $200. Their one-day annual factory clearance sale usually takes place at the end of April at the Victoria store, to coincide with their three-day extravaganza in Sidney.

Cheques, Credit cards

GEORGIA STRAIT OUTFITTERS
Mayfair Shopping Ctr, 300–3147 Douglas St (386-1080)
Royal Oak Shopping Ctr, 4448 W Saanich Rd (744-1706)
Hours: Mon, Tue & Sat 9:30–5:30; Wed–Fri 9:30–9; Sun noon–5

If your timing's on, the savings here can be extraordinary—more than 50% off recently: Insulated Tamaracks were going for $149.95 (down from $319.95)—in fact, every insulated jacket in the place was going for less than $200. A back-to-school sale offered students an extra 10% off, so that a $260 coat was going for $161.95. All sales final during discount period.

Cheques, Credit cards

GOLF PLUS +
3400 Douglas St (475-1886)
Hours: Mon, Tue & Sat 9:30–5:30; Wed–Fri 9:30–8; Sun noon–4

This sports store has a massive inventory, and when it's really eager to move stock, it has been known to offer the following: No GST or PST on shoes; 20% off clothing; $10 off any bag worth less than $100, and 20% off bags worth more. Major lines are Dexter, Callaway, Hogan, Mizuno, Nike, Ram, Spalding and Wilson.

Credit cards

HOGARTH SPORT & SKI
2122A Government St (480-1571; fax: 480-1572)
Hours: Mon–Th 9:30–6; Fri 9:30–9; Sat 9–5:30; Sun 11–5

They advertise "All the brands at low, low prices," and we've found them true to their word. There's a huge selection of brand-name skis, boots, snowboards, and sporting goods and equipment for every other season of the year. Free parking.

Cheques, Credit cards

HORSE CENTS CONSIGNMENT TACK STORE

Mill Bay: 1101 Shawnigan (743-8225)

Hours: Vary—call ahead

Used equestrian tack, riding boots and britches of all kinds are available here at low prices. Consigned goods are accepted during open hours (please call ahead); they even do blanket repairs.

Cheques

INTERNATIONAL KNIVES & DARTS

1306 Government St (383-2422; fax: 383-1247)

Hours: Mon 9–5:30; Tue–Th & Sat 9–7; Fri 9–9; Sun 10–4

Everything for the sports enthusiast in the way of cutting instruments—from diving and yachting knives to hunting and fishing knives. They also sharpen knives, chisels and scissors, supply Swiss army knife parts and pieces, and stock flashlights and other illuminating devices to make cutting easier. They have woodcarving tools and, of course, dart boards and arrows.

Cheques, Credit cards

ISLAND OUTFITTERS

740 Roderick St (475-4969; also fax)

Hours: Mon–Wed 9–6; Th & Fri 9–9; Sat 8–6; Sun 10–5

Bills itself as Victoria's "largest one-stop tackle shop." Most discounts seem to run 20 to 25% off regular retail—everything from float tubes to fishing vests to trout bait. Door crashers can be a "reel" bargain: A Shimano 100 GT Reel, regularly $59.99, went for $19.99—although there were only 35 of them in stock.

Credit cards

JEUNE BROS & PEETZ GREAT OUTDOORS STORE

570 Johnson St (386-8778; fax: 380-1533)

Hours: Mon–Th 9:30–6; Fri 9:30–9; Sat 9:30–5:30; Sun 11–5

The prices sure don't go back to this company's founding date—

1886—but given its location on one of Victoria's trendier shopping streets, the prices are surprisingly reasonable for fishing gear, sporting goods and assorted equipment for camping, hiking and climbing. There is always something clearance-priced in every category.

Credit cards

LAS VEGAS DISCOUNT GOLF & TENNIS
220– 777 Royal Oak Dr (727-9511; fax; 727-2511)
Hours: Mon–Wed & Sat 9:30–6; Th & Fri 9–9; Sun noon–5

This store sells clubs, racquets, clothing and sport supplies at a discount, and there's even a mini putting green where you can practise your "short game." Tennis brands include Head and Wilson, while golf names feature Spaulding, Ram and Wilson. They offer racquet re-stringing and periodic clear-out prices on discontinued golf shoes. Avail yourself of the free six-point club-and-swing check in their indoor "hitting room."

Cheques, Credit cards, InterAc

MARK'S WORK WEARHOUSE
3535 Ravine Way (383-7341)
Hours: Mon–Fri 9:30–9; Sat 9:30–5:30; Sun 11–5

A chain outlet where the stock in trade has always been durable work clothes and, in recent years, discounted denim fashion. The company's 100% cotton flannel shirts can go for $19.95, 80/20 wool and acrylic long underwear for $29.99 and Lee denim jackets for $69.99. A good place to load up on multi-packs of socks and briefs. Ample parking.

Credit cards

MICHEL'S CREATIVE WOODSHOP
Fisherman's Wharf, Finger #9 (479-9600)
Hours: Call ahead

Michel Richer specializes in wooden boat repairs, bright work, nautical carvings, trailboards and name plates for the sailing enthusiast. He also charters three-hour sails aboard his own vessel at $20 per person.

Cash preferred

NEVADA BOB'S DISCOUNT GOLF

205 – 3214 Douglas St (475-6177; fax: 475-3550)

Hours: Mon–Wed & Sat 9–6; Th & Fri 9–9; Sun 11–3

Our pal Cary prefers this place over other local discounters for what he terms "good prices and great customer service." The place itself boasts "the largest selection of golf clubs, shoes, bags and putters on Vancouver Island." Savings reflect about 50% off regular retail on golf sets, tennis balls, racquets and the Bobby Clampett spikeless Golf shoe (sale-priced last year for $62.88 with a free pair of socks thrown in for good measure). Sports clothing (Adidas and Top Seed, to name just two of the many top labels) is sometimes discounted 30-50% off. They also offer a free mail order catalogue. Easy wheelchair access.

Cheques, Credit cards

OCEAN RIVER SPORTS

1437 Store St (381-4233)

Hours: Mon–Th & Sat 9:30–5:30; Fri 9:30–8:30; Sun 11–5 (see text)

A good downtown outlet for new and used kayaks, canoes and apparel. Major lines include Current Designs, Royal Robbins, Patagonia, Merrell, White Hot and Outbound. When there's a manufacturer's clearance, discounts can be a much as 50%. They also fill mail orders. The rentals department is open Sun 9–5.

Cheques, Credit cards

PACIFIC TREKKING

1305 Government St (388-7088)

Hours: Mon–Sat 10–6; Sun noon–5

We've seen some extraordinary sales here—most notably Patagonia apparel up to 80% off. Other sales have discounted sportswear by 25 to 70%, boots by 20 to 30%, backpacks by up to 40%, and camping gear from 20 to 50%. Call for the dates of Pacific's swap meet rental sale, when you can trade used outdoor equipment for cash.

Cheques, Credit cards

SHANK'S SADDLERY
21408 Keating X Rd (652-2557)
Hours: Mon–Sat 9:30–6

Both English and Western-style equestrian supplies are available here, new and used, and on consignment. Call ahead to verify that they have riding helmets or boots in sizes you seek.

Cheques, Credit cards

SPORT MART DISCOUNT SUPERSTORES
Town & Country, 3593 Douglas St (475-6278)
Hours: Mon, Tue & Sat 9–6; Wed–Fri 9–9; Sun 10–5

A chain operation responding to the seasons—out with the bikes and in with the skis, then vice versa—and thus some great sales when the time comes to shift inventory. (We've seen TARGA R high performance slalom skis marked down to $199.88 from $625.) Shoe overstock can mean sales of up to 50% off for kids and adults—including Nike and Reebok.

Cheques, Credit cards, InterAc

SPORTS RENT
611 Discovery St (385-7368; same for fax)
Hours: Mon 8–6; Tue–Sat 9–6; Sun 10–6

A great find for the maybe-I'll-try-it enthusiast. This business enables you to try out a sport—and using better quality equipment than a beginner can usually afford—for a fraction of the cost to buy. Sport Rent also sells both new and used rollerblades (their specialty) and accessories, surf boards, wet suits, snow boards, and complete ski packages.

Cheques, Credit cards, InterAc

SPORTS TRADERS
508 Discovery St (383-6443)
Hours: Mon–Fri 9:30–6; Sat 9–6; Sun 10:30–4:30

By all accounts, a good place to take equipment you have outgrown or outpaced. In return, this is a good place to pick up used equipment: Rowers, bikes and treadmills have been available for as little as $49. At season's end, skiwear and equipment was 50% off. Trade-ins are welcome. Extensive aerobic and workout wear. Handicapped access. Ample parking.

Cheques, Credit cards, InterAc

STEVENSON'S SHOE CLINIC (repair runners)—See Shoes & Footwear

TROTAC MARINE
85 Dallas Rd (386-2341)
Hours: Mon–Fri 8:30–5; Sat 9–2

Right next to Ogden Point, we found this family-run operation, a source for lamps, barometers, brass clocks and other quality ship's fittings, alongside books, calendars and cruising guides, plus Mustang flotation wear. Prices are low.

Cash only

VINTAGE HOT TUBS (beds, too)—See Bedding

WILD BIRDS NATURE SHOP
20–797 Hillside Ave (480-1600)
Hours: Mon–Sat 10–6; Sun noon–5

A wonderful assortment of items to attract and entertain wild birds—and some great gifts for bird-watchers, kids and country living. There are feeders, seed, birdhouses, books, videos, gift items, children's items and lots of free advice about seasonal feeding of our winged friends.

Cheques, Credit cards

TOYS, PAPER PRODUCTS, PERSONAL STATIONERY & PARTY SUPPLIES

EARTHBORNE ART & PAPERWORKS
1608 Camosun St (383-0144)
Hours: Fri & Sat 11–5 or by appt.

This tiny gallery sells fibre arts, handmade paper and gifts at very reasonable prices. There are books, journals, stationery, and gift cards created by several local artisans. Note weekend hours only, or by appointment.

Cheques

FLAMINGOS BY YARD CARDS
Address unavailable (727-6616)
Hours: 24 hour answering machine

Want to surprise a friend with 30 pink flamingoes on the front lawn? This outfit will do the job for a meagre $45 (in Victoria). Prices rise to about $65 the further they have to travel out of Victoria to place (and later retrieve) the birds. Each "event" is accompanied by a giant cartoon sign.

Cheques

FLAMINGO RENTALS & MORE
Address unavailable (595-7465)
Hours: 24 hour referral to cellular phone

Another outfit for embarrassing and humiliating your closest friends when a milestone birthday approaches, this one charges about $50 (on average) and also can supply buzzards instead of the traditional tacky birds.

Cheques

GALA-VAN PARTY RENTALS
101 Burnside Rd W (383-5431; fax: 383-5331)
Hours: Mon–Th & Sat 9–5; Fri 9–9

Everything you need to rent for entertaining—cutlery, glasses, plates, tablecloths, even party tents—at low cost. Call for estimate.

Credit cards

KABOODLES
1320 Government St (383-0931)
Hours: Mon–Th & Sat 10–6; Fri 10–9; Sun noon–5

Here's our favourite stop for stocking-stuffers, party favours and modest gifts that say "I thought of you" instead of "I've got lots of cash to splurge." We particularly like their assortment of small gifts for under $1, stickers, candies and novelties. And of course, they have wondrous costumes, wigs, wands, Dracula teeth and the like for dress up or Hallowe'en.

Cheques, Credit cards

SEEING IS BELIEVING

564 Johnson St (383-5880)

Hours: Mon–Sat 9:30–5:30; Sun noon–5

Mayfair Mall, 3147 Douglas St (361-3551)

Hours: Mon, Tue & Sat 9:30–5:30; Wed–Fri 9:30–9; Sun noon–5

Billing themselves as the source for "possible gifts for impossible people," these shops offer great browsing, and small gifts from 25 cents to sky's-the-limit. Hi-tech gifts and gadgets are nearly irresistible, but fortunately, selected items are always 50% off. The Mayfair store just opened last spring.

Credit cards

TOY TRADERS

516 Herald St (480-5541)

Hours: Mon–Fri 9:30–5:30; Sat 10–6; Sun noon–4

Associated with Sports Traders, these folks seek any and all toys (in good condition), suitable for infant to age 12. They buy, sell, trade and consign anything they can get their hands on. They have computer games like Nintendo, and older systems like Turbo-Grafix, Intellivision and Atari, plus tons of board games, ride-on toys, cribs and strollers and adventure playground equipment—in short, anything other people's kids may have outgrown. Naturally, everything is dirt cheap to buy. This is where we sold our old Nintendo system. Nice folks and a pleasant, unrushed atmosphere.

Cheques, Credit cards

THE TOYBOX TOY LIBRARY

Vic West "Y", 521 Craigflower Rd (382-9514)

Hours: Tue 3–5; Wed 1–noon; Sat 10–12:30

Membership costs a modest $30 (plus 6 volunteer hours) per year, entitling you to share in the hundreds of toys available for loan from this Vic West play program. Imagine what you'd otherwise spend for toys in a year.

Cheques

UNICEF STORE
2230 Oak Bay Ave (598-9922)
Hours: Mon–Fri 9–4; Sat 10–4

Stationery, cards and gift items are sold here at modest prices, and you'll have the bonus of knowing your dollars go to Third World countries to help save lives. There are also educational games and toys and cards for occasions other than the usual Unicef Christmas period. Call for free catalogue.

Cash preferred

ZYDECO
565 Johnson St (389-1877)
Hours: Mon–Sat 10–5:30; Sun noon–5

Certainly one of our favourite "toy" stores (we say it that way because there are play things for grownups, too). We drop in half the time just to visit with the irrepressible Harry Roet (he's usually off golfing Wednesday and Thursday, by the way), who's obviously a kid who never grew up—and loves it that way. (Ask to see his original Woodstock tickets, which he has kept in his wallet for 25 years.) There's "fridge fun": Magnet words for kids, families, sweethearts, gays, secretaries, college students and dieters. There's the glow-in-the-dark human skeleton puzzle ("educational, too," chimes in Harry). There are great T-shirts—like Roy Troll fish homages and lots of cows. And there are perfect pinata-stuffers: Toys by the scoop—old fashioned plastic miniatures for $1.25 a scoop. Zydeco turns over its entire stock of coloured lights every six weeks, simply because their prices are cheaper than anywhere else. Strings of cows, cactus, bacon-and-eggs, flamingoes, or Harry's personal favourites—those Maxfield Parrish-hued moons—sell for $29.95 a strand. Says Harry: "Once you get one strand, you get wired—literally." Accordingly, he provides mail order (postal code is V8W 1M2) for those who simply must have more lights but can't get to the store.

Credit cards

ARTS & CRAFTS SUPPLIES

ARTISTS STUDIO TOUR
1040 Moss St (384-4101)
Hours: Usually Sun 11–4

The volunteer committee to Art Gallery of Greater Victoria hosts its annual tour of top local artists' studios, usually held on the last Sunday of March. Tickets may be purchased at the Gallery in advance of the tour itself (call for details as tour date approaches). The big deal here is that people who attend may purchase works of art directly from the featured artists, at savings of about 40–50% off usual gallery prices.

Cheques

EASTERN INTERIORS
572 Fisgard St (385-4643)
Hours: Daily 9:30–6; closed for lunch noon–1

We found authentic Chinese giftwares here, including inexpensive chops, ink stones ($5.99 to $7.99), large astrology chops at $12.99 (about 50% cheaper than prices in Vancouver), art supplies, bonsai books, brushes and large porcelain pots—all inexpensive.

Credit cards

OPUS FRAMING & ART SUPPLIES
1627 Store St (386-8133; fax: 386-8999)
Hours: Mon–Sat 9:30–5:30; Sun 1–5

Opus is a discount fine artists' materials store featuring one of the largest paper selections in Western Canada. It's an easy-access, self-serve environment that encourages customers to browse in search of new and exciting products to spark their creativity. Opus's specialties are fine art papers, canvas, paints and brushes, all at near-wholesale prices.

Cheques, Credit cards, InterAc

SEWING SUPPLIES

FABRIC 'N' FASHIONS
Saanichton: Pioneer Village, 4 – 7816 East Saanich (652-6322)
Hours: Mon–Sat 9:30–5:30

Quality fabrics and notions are carried in vast array here, with the focus on European imports and patterns. Their winter clearance offers exceptional values on selected stock. Cheques accepted only for customers on their mailing list—inquire at store.

Cheques, Credit cards

FABRICLAND
201 – 3400 Douglas St (475-7501; fax: 475-7502)
851 Johnson St (381-2411)
Hours: Mon–Wed 9:30–6; Th & Fri 9:30–9; Sat 9:30–5:30; Sun noon–5

Within every Fabricland store, there's now a "Home Dec Depot" —a specialty home-decorating centre with free ideas and everyday values. The big deal for us at Fabricland has always been its Sewing Club, with added discounts for members and a jump on periodic sales. Membership costs $5 if you join mid-year or $10 for a calendar year (Jan–Dec). Seniors who are members get additional discounts on Wednesday and Thursday. The Sewing Club Members' Value Hotlines are 475-7503 or 385-SALE for regularly updated recordings about special prices.

Cheques, Credit cards

FANNY'S FABRICS
3090 Nanaimo St (388-5132; Yarn Store: 388-4402)
406 – 3980 Shelbourne St (477-8494)
Hours: Mon–Fri 9:30–9; Sat 9–5:30; Sun noon–5 (both)

One of our favourite stops at Fanny's is the "Fabric Value" clearance centre at the back, where remnants are priced as low as two for 94 cents. The downtown location is a big, bright store, though staff are what we'd call "leisurely," so there's almost always a queue at the till. We like the large assortment of yarn in the knitting area at the back. Please also see below for "Singer Sewing Centre" entry.

Credit cards

FOUR SEASONS FABRICS
650 View St (384-0561)
Hours: Mon–Sat 9–5:30

Always worth a browse for quilting remnants or periodic sales; we've found cotton denim here in 60-inch widths for 30% off.

Credit cards

GREATEST KNITS
1294 Gladstone Ave (386-5523)
Hours: Tue–Sat 9:30–5:30

In addition to their regular knitting supplies and periodic sales, the drawing card here is the Wednesday-night (7–9 p.m.) drop-in class for all levels of experience.

Cheques, Credit cards

SATIN MOON QUILT SHOP
Market Square, 517 Pandora Ave (383-4023)
Hours: Mon–Th & Sat 9:30–5:30; Fri 9:30–9; Sun 11–5

Often what we want most here is priced beyond our budget, but there are always 30%-off clearance shelves for samples and remnants (and small quilt cuts we can't resist, even at full price). As well, their post holiday clearance wares are usually discounted a full 50% off—everything from material to books and patterns, to sample quilts themselves.

Credit cards

SAWYER SEWING CENTRE
840 Fort St (388-6228)
Hours: Mon–Fri 8–5:30; Sat 9–5

All their sewing machine service is guaranteed, and they promise one-day repairs: "In by 9, out by 5." They carry top brand names—new and used—on domestic and industrial machines, as well as new and used sergers. They have a standing offer to buy any industrial machines for cash. Trade-ins welcome. Demonstration and discontinued models sold off cheaply. Scissors and serger blades sharpened. Free parking behind store.

Credit cards

SEW TECH SEWING CENTRE
1900 Store St (384-4404)
Hours: Mon–Sat 9–5:30; Sun 10–4

Sidney: 2353 Bevan Ave (656-3373)
Hours: Mon–Sat 9–5:30

Located inside Capital Iron, these sales and service departments offer mobile repair service, reconditioned machines, sharpening, financing and leasing—and they welcome trade-ins. They carry top-line brands like Bernina and have periodic clear-outs of fabric, notions and remnants.

Cheques, Credit cards

SEW-CHEAP NOTIONS
660 Discovery St (360-1135)
Hours: Mon–Fri 9:30–4:30; Sat 9:30–1

This place offers regular discounts on something every week, and we've generally found it to be the best source for notions in town. Typical discounts on sale items average 30% off on everything from craft batts to hand-sewing needles, to those wonderful Ghinger applique scissors, to cutting mats and pattern boards. Craft laces were recently sale-priced at 12 yards for just $1.50. Owner Charles Hitchens knows everything about sewing notions—he even told us where to find old-fashioned hat forms from Stern's, a competitor in Vancouver.

Cheques

SINGER DEALER CENTRE
3090B Nanaimo St (383-6141)
Hours: Mon–Wed 9:30–6; Th & Fri 9:30–9; Sat 9–5

Here, inside Fanny's Fabrics, is the authorized Singer factory service centre for the Island—sales, service and parts and expert repairs to all makes and models of sewing machines and sergers.

They sell reconditioned machines and 220-volt machines for industrial use, and they welcome trade-ins. Easy wheelchair access.

Credit cards

SOUVENIRS

CANADIANA DISCOUNT GIFTS AND SOUVENIRS
1012 Government St (384-3123)
Hours: Daily 9–5:30

Mountie dolls? Flags? Hand-carved totem poles, plaques and masks? Here's the place. We found authentic Cowichan sweaters, regularly $144.95 for just $71.95, leather gloves for $10 and carved totems discounted to $50 from $99. As souvenir shops go, this one has some genuine savings. They also stock B.C. jade and rhodonite, a wide selection of adult and children's moccasins, aboriginal jewellery and soapstone carvings and a vast selection of T-shirts and sweatshirts.

Credit cards

JULIE'S COTTAGE CRAFTS—See Decorative Accessories

ORIENTAL BOOK & GIFT—See Decorative Accessories

OUT OF HAND GALLERY—See Decorative Accessories

RAINBOW MAYA SHOP (blown glass)—See Alternative Clothing

THE WILDLIFE STORE—See Alternative Clothing

WINGS WILDLIFE NATURE BOUTIQUE—See Alternative Clothing

TRAVEL

Considerable travel deals can be had if you are flexible in terms of departure or return dates and times; by way of the most extreme example, if you're willing to leave tomorrow, you can sometimes call today and get a last-minute ticket that an agent is desperate to unload. Early morning, late evening or midweek travel is often cheaper than weekend, and there are usually discounts for seniors (see B.C. Ferries for an example of both.)

AIR B.C.
1000 Wharf St (360-9074)
Hours: 24 hour (or answering machine, off hours)

Cheap early-morning weekday flights are available through Air B.C. on the Vancouver-Victoria and Vancouver-Nanaimo routes. Call for latest discount and scheduling information. When we went to press, the cost was only $30 one-way.

Credit cards

B.C. FERRIES
Head office, 1112 Fort St (381-1401)
General information: 386-3431
Recorded information: 656-0757
Hours: Daily 24 hrs (last number only)

B.C. seniors travel free as foot passengers, Monday through Thursday on most routes. Discount rates are available for groups of 15 or more, travelling together, as walk-on passengers, or in one vehicle—book at least 7 days in advance. On weekends, the buffet on the Super-ferries is an excellent value. If you travel on the Victoria Line ferry from downtown Victoria (Ogden Point) to downtown Seattle (Pier 48), a round-trip ticket can save you a bit: Car and driver $49 one-way, $90 return. (See Victoria-Seattle ferry entry below.) For details from outside the free-calling area, call Tourism Victoria at 1-800-663-3883 for details.

Credit cards (at most terminals), or cash

CRUISE CONNECTIONS
Address unavailable (1-800-661-WAVE)
Hours: Mon–Fri 6–6; Sat & Sun 7–4

A 24-hour cruise hot-line (1-684-9282) and excellent periodic seat-sale-style deals: A recent promotion offered a free cellular phone with the purchase of any cruise package.

Credit cards

GODFREY'S LUGGAGE & LEATHER REPAIRS & SALES
2508 Douglas St (388-5262)
Hours: Tue–Sat 8:30–5

There's a 50%-off clearance periodically on leather bags and 20–30% off purses, and usually, there's an entire table here of discounts from 50–75% off, too. Reliable repairs to all your luggage.

Cash only

HOTELROOM CLEARANCE CENTER
Address unavailable (1-800-662-2940)
Hours: Mon–Fri 9–5:30

Great discounts on hotel packages for rooms in Anaheim, Seattle, Portland, Friday Harbor, Vancouver, San Francisco, Phoenix, San Diego and other destinations. (Note its weekdays-only hours.) Canadian dollars are converted to U.S. when you book, so be sure to confirm the final amount you'll be expected to pay. Prices quoted are about 50% off regular rack rates and usually apply to two nights and two people (extra nights usually available on a prorated basis).

Credit cards

THE LAST MINUTE CLUB
201–1290 Broad Street (380-4888, 1-800-663-1559; fax: 385-1499)
Hours: Daily, 24 hours (answering machine during off-hours)

Big-ticket tour packages are substantially reduced by booking through this branch of Pacific Rim Travel Corporation, but they really mean it when they say last-minute. If you book far in advance, you pay full price.

Credit cards

OAK BAY EXPLORER
Address unavailable (598-4556)
Hours: Mon–Sat 10–4 (summers only)

This free, double-decker bus operates from May to September to convey passengers on a circle tour from points in downtown Victoria to points in Oak Bay Village. Pickup locations downtown (mainly in the Inner Harbour area) include the Coho Ferry; Admiral's Hotel; Harbour Towers Hotel; and the Empress. Stops in or near Oak Bay include the Oak Bay Rec Centre; Oak Bay Ave and Foul Bay Rd; the Oak Bay Beach Hotel; the Oak Bay Marina, Willows Beach; Estevan Beach; Oak Bay Village; and the Blethering Place. The last is one of a number of local businesses about which a thumbnail history is given in a free Oak Bay Explorer booklet available at Travel B.C. (the Travel InfoCentre is across from the Empress, just up from Milestones), which also includes complete schedule information.

Free

TOURISM VICTORIA
Travel InfoCentre, 812 Wharf St (382-2127; fax: 382-6539)
Hours: Daily 9–8

We love this free service and are indebted to Media & Public Relations Manager Heather Day for her invaluable assistance in finding little tidbits of info for us. She even walked over to Fan Tan Alley one day to dig up the name of a business we were having trouble locating. Any questions you might have about travel to (or within) the Victoria area can be answered here—and we've asked them some doozies. Very helpful, resourceful and friendly folks.

Free

TRAVEL CUTS
Finerty Rd/Student Union Bld, U.Vic (721-6916, 721-8352)
Hours: Mon–Fri 9:30–5

They supply students with Eurail passes and products, as well as point-to-point reservations, cheap accommodation arrangements and various youth passes, all at discount prices, of course. Cheques are accepted only if tendered two weeks in advance of travel.

Cheques (see text), Credit cards

VICTORIA CLIPPER
Address unavailable (382-8100)
Hours: Daily, 24 hours (or machine during off-hours)

We find their regular rates a bit steep, but their excursion rates to Seattle are a real deal—and some can be added to excellent-value hotel packages. Again, we recommend the return fare price to save a little.

Credit cards

VICTORIA-SEATTLE FERRY
185 Dallas Rd (480-5544)
Hours: Mon–Fri 9–5; reservations Daily 6:30 a.m–6:30 p.m. (see text)

Reservations are available by calling 480-5555 or fax 480-5222. Recorded information is at 1-800-668-1167. If you need to call Canada Customs before departing, the number is 363-3531. We find the price of this trip a little dear at $49 (car and driver) each way, but it's improved if you book return tickets at $90 (Cdn). Still, when you consider the cost of travelling to Seattle via ferry to Tsawwassen, and then driving down to the States, with gas and time expended, it's probably a deal after all. In any case, it's a pleasant four-hour voyage, but we frankly recommend you bring your food: At press time, the mediocre breakfast buffet cost $8, with no price reduction for children. (At least there's a Starbucks cappuccino bar on board.) Kids of all ages will like the impressive video arcade, where the games accept Canadian quarters.

Credit cards, Travellers' cheques only

WESTERN TRAVEL
729 Johnson St (382-6160)
Hours: Mon–Fri 9–5; Sat 10–3

A whole range of ever-changing travel bargains are offered by this reputable business, which has been serving Victoria residents since 1945. Call to find out what's on the roster in coming weeks. Free parking in the parkade opposite.

Credit cards

TELECOMMUNICATIONS, PAGERS, ETC.

CAM-NET
200, 885 Dunsmuir St, Vancouver (1-800-688-9733; fax: 1-684-0638)

Hours: Daily, 24 hours (off-hours, call 1-689-0800 or the 800 number for customer service)

A boon to anyone who uses long distance, even casually, Cam-Net regularly saves us 20–50% on all our domestic long distance bills. Sign-up fee of $10 is periodically waived to attract new customers, and a nominal monthly charge ($1 or $2) may apply if you don't use the service at all for a month or so. Available currently only in major city centres (ie. in Victoria, Vancouver, Toronto, but not on Salt Spring Island, for instance), Cam-Net uses U.S. routing to save on calls even within Canada. International calls still save 10%.

Cheques

DIAL DIRECT PAGING
1420 Quadra St (361-1210; fax: 360-1741)

Hours: Daily, 24 hours (of course)

At press time, they were offering a brand-name pager for $88, including eight months' free airtime, eight months' free voice mail and no activation fee, so you can join the ranks of those annoying people whose pagers go off mid-movie. Just kidding: This unit features "Mem-O-Lert," a silent alerting voice message retention.

Monthly invoices payable by cheques

INTERCONNECT BUSINESS SYSTEMS
3578 Quadra St (384-0511)

Hours: Mon–Fri 9–noon and 1–5

Two-day service on most telephone and answering machine repairs. A new battery for our portable phone cost only $18 (compared to almost twice as much elsewhere) and a new circuit for our static-ridden B.C. Tel phone cost $24 to fix (compared to $40 we were quoted in Vancouver).

Credit cards

UNITEL COMMUNICATIONS
Address unavailable (384-6651; 1-800-733-3900)
Hours: Daily till 11 p.m. (24 hour messaging)

There's no fee to sign up for Unitel. You are promised savings of 15% off B.C. Tel long-distance charges, or 28% with a special plan for one number of your choice. So, if you like to call your folks in P.E.I. every Sunday and chat for 20 minutes, this'll save you plenty. You can get monthly overseas discounts for $3 per month and your Unitel card is good for use anywhere in Canada, except the three prairie provinces, Yukon and N.W.T. Simply call the 800 number to sign up.

Cheques

PETS

BORDEN MERCANTILE COMPANY
3960 Borden St (479-2084; 479-3414)
Hours: Mon–Sat 8–5:30

Deals aplenty here on pet foods, dog and cat toys, birdseed and many items in the gardening and craft areas (such as kid-size gardening tools and candle-making supplies).

Cheques, Credit cards

THE CHOW BARN
784 Spruce Ave (382-4484)
Hours: Mon–Sat 9–6; Sun noon–5

Oak Bay: 2185 Theatre Lane (595-5224)
Hours: Mon–Fri 9:30–5:30; Sat 9:30–5

Pet food and supplies are sold here at modest prices; periodic sales are advertised in the newspapers for even bigger savings.

Cheques, Credit cards

THE FEED BARN
10223 McDonald Park Rd (655-4433)
Hours: Mon–Sat 9–5:30

Just north of Slegg Lumber, you'll find Mary-Anne LaBoucan's store, which offers everyday values on domestic pet food, livestock feed, wild bird seed and several lines of therapeutic pet foods. Say hi to Mary-Anne's English springer spaniel, Cleo, when you visit.

Cheques, Credit cards

MUCKY MUTT PET EMPORIUM
222 – 2950 Douglas St (384-5224)
Brentwood: 7159C West Saanich Rd (652-2610)
Hours: Mon 9:30–5:30; Tue–Sat 7:30–5:30; Sun noon–4

Really friendly staff make using these facilities fun—even if you weren't saving money. The bargain here is in do-it-yourself pet washing and grooming—a quick, comfortable and affordable way to bathe your pet. Also for sale are pet accessories and wellness products.

Cheques, Credit cards

NOTES:

3. CLOTHING

DISCOUNT, OFF-PRICE STORES AND SAMPLE SHOPS

BAGGINS
540 Johnson St (388-7022)
Hours: Mon–Sat 10–5:30; Sun 11–5:30

A bright, large and stylish shop for teens and young women, Baggins always has a 50%-off rack out front on the sidewalk, and another at the very back of the store. Trendy fashions include Hollywood jeans and original clothing designs by Anokki for Sarah Clothes. Most attire is in natural fibres of rayon or 100% cotton.

Credit cards

COTTONS & BLUES
Sidney: 2437 Beacon Ave (656-6933)
Hours: Mon–Sat 9:30–5:30; Sun noon–5

There's always a sale rack here, and periodically overstock reduction sales offer discounts up to 75% off regular retail. Examples of bargains: Discontinued aerobic wear, manufacturer's clearance of name-brand jeans, end-of-lines casual shoes and blow-out prices on summer separates like activewear and shorts. During clearance periods, all sales are final.

Cheques, Credit cards

L.A. CONNECTION
Mayfair Shopping Centre, 216–3147 Douglas St (381-3454)
Hours: Mon, Tue & Sat 9:30–5:30; Wed–Fri 9:30–9; Sun noon–5

The store's periodic sales qualify for entry in our book, particularly the annual back-to-school blue jeans trade: Your old pair—regardless of how thrashed and trashed they might be—will bring you a $10 discount on any pair of new jeans.

Cheques, Credit cards

PIZZAZZ
2234 Oak Bay Ave (592-4432)
Hours: Mon–Sat 9:30–5:30; Sun noon–5

There's a special sale in casual women's wear and high fashion almost every week at Pizzazz, but our favourite is probably the Hallowe'en Spectacular Week, which offers "daily in-store specials at fantastic spooky prices." Stock turns over rapidly at this location, so it's wise to drop in whenever you're in the neighbourhood to see what's marked down that week.

Credit cards

THE SWEATER BOX
Nootka Court, 19a–633 Courtney St (380-0830)
Hours: Mon–Sat 10–5, Sun (summer only) noon–5

Owner Sheryl Gilding boasts that her "unique sweaters are like works of art," which would explain the generally steep prices. The real deal is the "Sweater Punch Card," which allows you to buy five sweaters (or group together your mom, friends and relatives to buy five), and then you get your next sweater—regardless of price—for 50% off. Says Sheryl, "It's a way of getting those $380 sweaters you'd never be able to afford for half price." In addition, she lets interested customers host home parties where her fine sweaters are for sale; the hostess can earn a discount (of between 5 and 10%) on the total sales of the evening, which may then be applied to any sweater from the shop.

Cheques, Credit cards

WORKWEAR WORLD
Broadmead Village, 210–777 Royal Oak Dr (744-1777; fax: 744-2122)
CanWest Shopping Centre, 110–2945 Jacklin Rd (474-1930)
Mayfair Shopping Centre, 291 Mayfair Ctr (386-3131)
Tillicum Mall, 55–3170 Tillicum Rd (386-6565)
University heights, 401–3980 Shelbourne St (477-3800)
Sidney: 1B–9764 5th St (656-1970)
Hours: Mall hours, or call ahead

We've always relied on the down-to-earth atmosphere of Workwear World, and their stable stock of practical, hard-wearing clothing, footwear and accessories. They generally stock both Lee and Levis jeans, Pioneer rainwear, Hi-Tec boots, Polar Paws socks, and other solid, brand names, all at really low prices. Good quality flannel shirts are almost always sale priced at $9.99, and we found a fine winter jacket from Lee's Storm Rider label (tough, durable denim lined with cosy Sherpa pile) for only $59.99.

Credit cards

FACTORY & MANUFACTURERS' OUTLETS & CLEARANCE CENTRES

BREEZE
1150 Government St (383-8871)
Hours: Mon, Tue & Sat 10–6; Wed–Fri 10–9; Sun noon–6

Esprit is still a label highly prized for superior fit and wearability, yet we rarely see it discounted in Victoria. Breeze, however, runs periodic one-cent sales (buy one, get a second for just 1 cent) featuring top-selling Esprit pants and T-shirts. One of these sales is regularly scheduled, (while supplies last), at back-to-school-time.

Credit cards

COOK DESIGN STUDIOS
2616 Bridge St (384-4871; fax: 384-3224)
Hours: Sat & Sun only 10–5

This wholesale source of fashion and team sportswear, stonewashed jeans and T-shirts offers over 100 designs and custom screened printing at about half what you'd pay elsewhere. Discount membership is available in their "Almost Wholesale Club," which enables you to buy at factory-direct prices. Please note the factory outlet is open weekends only.

Cheques

ELLEY'S LEATHER
Market Square, 560 Johnson St (383-7834)
Hours: Mon–Sat 10–5

Elley's holds periodic sales and always discounts some of their fine leathers at prices up to 50% off regular retail. Some examples: Bolero-length leather jackets for women at $149, leather skirts at $49.50 (compare to $135) and men's blazer-style jackets for only $99 (regularly $500). Lines and sizes are broken during clear-out periods, so it's strictly first-come, first-served, with no layaways.

Credit cards

KIDS ONLY CLOTHING CLUB
Address unavailable (652-9695)
Hours: Mon–Sat 9–5

Call Glenda Bilinsky for a free catalogue for the current season and find out how you can earn free clothing by hosting a "Kids Only" home party. In any event, you'll find savings by buying direct. Stock includes 100% Canadian-made mix and match coordinates for kids—and moms, too. Most designs for children are 100% durable cotton with adjustable waists, grow-cuffs and knee patches.

Cheques

THE LEATHER RANCH
302 – Victoria Eaton Centre (384-4217)
Hours: Mon–Wed & Sat 9:30–5:30; Th & Fri 9:30–9; Sun noon–5

This well-known manufacturer sells direct to the public at prices that—for the quality—are 25 to 50% off retail. Choose from full-length coats, jackets, slacks, skirts, pants and Western-style fringed jackets for kids. Most are stylishly casual, some even dressy, and there's a limited range of accessories.

Credit cards

MYSTIC LANE SHIRT CO.
1007 Langley St (380-6452)
Hours: Call for appointment

This wholesale T-shirt supplier stocks mainly 100% cotton, and specializes in custom screen printing. There's a 24-unit minimum on orders, whether screened or not, and the discount is approximately 50% off retail.

Cheques

NARNIA WEAR
1670 Warren Gardens (595-6789; or pager 360-4668)
Hours: Daily 9–5

Honey Palm represents a line of Canadian-made, 100% cotton children's wear that can be bought from her directly, or via home parties. As usual, the home party hostess can receive a percentage of sales in the form of a credit against other merchandise from the line. Some adult wear is available, too, such as their luxurious cotton terry robes.

Cheques

OUT OF THE BLUE SPORTSWEAR
10 – 626 Esquimalt Rd (380-9179)
Hours: Mon–Fri 9–5; Sat, call ahead

Here's a true wholesale outlet, which means: Don't ask for assistance while they're dealing with a retail customer, and please also call ahead to make sure they're not too busy when you plan to visit. They make up bulk orders, so there's a 12-item minimum—

but you'll save 50% over comparable retail. Out of the Blue will custom-screen on the garments. Among the on-hand stock are T's, jackets, corporate uniforms and casual clothing.

Cheques

SAVE ON SHIRTS
2605 Bridge St (383-8115; fax: 383-8677)
Hours: M–F 9–5:30; Sat 10–3

A true wholesale outlet, this place manufactures T-shirts, sweats and caps, and can outfit teams or individuals; no minimum order is required, but the price goes down as the quantities increase. They have a big selection of colours and styles, and they can custom-screen or add crests for teams.

Cheques

VALHALLA OUTFITTERS
615 Broughton St (360-2181)
Hours: Mon–Th & Sat 9:30–6; Fri 9:30–9; Sun 11–5:30

This line of high-quality outerwear is priced for the peak of their market, but they are Victoria's sole factory outlet store, as far as we can tell. Expect savings of 50% off retail, although, as we said, they start out rather pricey. Periodic sale prices are quite good: storm jackets for $70 (regularly $120), insulated parkas at $100 and in-store specials discounted up to 70%. The "Snap-T" and "Full-Zip" jackets are particularly well-made—they use only the best "no-pill" polar fleece. Good value on their tights, which have insulating properties not found in cheaper lines.

Credit cards

WOW WALL TO WALL KIDS
Address unavailable (477-5734 or 744-2222)
Hours: Mon–Fri 9–5

Kids' and moms' fashions and accessories are sold by Jodi Noble (first phone number, above) and Michelle Barkley (second number) on a home-party or buy-direct basis at discounts of about 50% off retail. Clothing is high quality, catalogues are free, and there's a 100% money-back guarantee of satisfaction and two-day delivery.

Cheques

CONSIGNMENT

CLOTHESLINE CLOTHING CO.

Saanich: 4488 West Saanich Rd (479-0800)

Hours: Mon–Sat 10–5

"Clothes kids love to wear at prices Mom can afford," is the self-proclaimed credo of Clothesline Clothing, and they're right. Unlike many consignment shops we've seen, this one is well-organized and fashionable, and the kids' clothing is in like-new condition. Clothesline also carries a line of their own children's garments and charming hats. Your consignment items are seen just about anytime during normal business hours—except Saturdays—but you should call ahead anyway to find out what they're seeking before venturing out.

Cheques, Credit cards

DESIGNER CONSIGNOR

106 – 1315 Esquimalt Rd (380-0021)

Hours: Mon–Sat 10:30–5

Your consignment goods are seen here anytime during open hours. Stock runs the gamut from women's attire, earrings, purses and shoes, to children's clothing and toys. They also usually have a good selection of maternity wear, which we've found difficult to track down in other stores. Ask for Debbie, the owner, when you call ahead to see what she's buying, or what kind of current stock they have on hand to sell. Don't overlook the 99-cent rack outside.

Cheques

ELAN FASHION COLLECTIONS

102 – 1841 Oak Bay Ave (598-5331)

Hours: Tue–Fri 9:30–4:30; Sat 9:30–4

As you might expect from this Oak Bay Village location, the stock at Elan is very upmarket and styles are current. Call ahead to make sure that the owner, Margaret, is there to view your clean, in-season garments. Your consigned clothing need not be designer label, but Elan does cater to business women, so it's best to focus on suits, bags and good shoes. Margaret prefers natural fibres and always rates "good styling" as most suitable for her discerning clientele.

Cheques, Credit cards

THE FASHION CYCLE
1048 Fort St (384-2299)
Hours: Mon–Fri 10–5; Sat 11–5

The emphasis at Fashion Cycle is on current season attire and natural fibres. They will see your high quality cast-offs anytime except on Saturdays, but again, it's always wise to call ahead to see what they think sells best.

Cheques

FRUGAL FASHIONS
1103 & 1105 Oscar St (385-2500)
Hours: Mon–Sat 10–5

This boutique-style consignment shop occupies a charming white house at the corner of Cook and Oscar. Your consignment is seen only by appointment Monday to Wednesday, usually only between 10:30 am and 4:30 pm, so call the owner, Karen, to set up a time. Karen offers the standard 50-50 split to her consignors. Stock includes menswear, women's and children's clothing (the latter including infant and toddler wear), plus clean toys, books and giftware, much of it new.

Cheques

HORSE CENTS CONSIGNMENT TACK STORE—See Recreation

HOUSE OF SAVOY—See Vintage

MY SISTER'S CLOSET
Fairfield Plaza, 1548 Fairfield Rd (598-2421)
Hours: Mon–Sat 10–5:30; Sun variable

Unlike Elan, mentioned above, this place defiantly avoids career wear and anything dressy or "fussy". The primary focus is women's clothing, shoes, and accessories—perferably vests, gauzy skirts and cute back-to-basics looks. The consignor gets a 50-50 split with the shop. Your goods are seen from 10 am to 5 pm weekdays only, and they ask that all tendered items be fresh, current styles and clean.

Cheques, Credit cards

THE NEARLY NEW SHOP
3631 Shelbourne St (477-5821)
Hours: Mon–Sat 10–5:30

Every woman who must wear a uniform for technical work will treasure this find: A real consignment outlet for nurses, dental assistants and the like. Consignments are received Monday through Wednesday from 10 am to 2 pm only, and the split is approximately 50-50 with the consignor; they actually quote you the price they'll pay you when the garment sells, then they double it and add 50 cents to achieve the final selling price. If you're in the market to buy or sell a uniform, this shop is unique in Victoria, and the prices are very reasonable.

Credit cards, Cheques

NICE TWICE CONSIGNMENT SHOP—See Maternity & Children's Wear

THE OLDE FASHION HOUSE
1971 Oak Bay Ave (598-9932)
Hours: Tue–Sat 10:30–5

Owner Vinnie Chadwick carries mostly women's clothing here on consignment. Outfits run the gamut from casual to career, and all are of better quality. The standard 50-50 split is offered for your consigned goods, and Vinnie will view them anytime during open hours, although she can't always price them right then; if things are hectic, leave the clothes and she'll get back to you.

Cheques, credit cards

PANDORA'S CLOSET
Sidney: 9783 3rd St (656-6421)
Hours: Mon–Sat 10–4:30

High fashion women's clothing is carried on consignment here, but since the ownership changed in June 1994, hours may have changed too, so call ahead.

Cheques, Credit cards

PLAY IT AGAIN
2000 Fernwood Rd (380-0049)
Hours: Mon–Sat 10:30–5

This beautiful shop looks exactly like a fashionable boutique: Inside walls are natural grey brick, there's a small, scrupulously clean changing room, and the "funky, casual and classic" garments are displayed with the kind of attention to detail usually reserved for designer frocks in a fancy showroom. But first impression are deceptive; instead, Play it Again turns out to be a consignment shop. Outside, there's a $5 rack, and against one inside wall everything's $10. Consigned goods are seen by appointment only.

Cheques, Credit cards, InterAc

REPEAT PERFORMANCE
2017 Oak Bay Ave (595-5432)
Hours: Mon–Th 10–5; Fri & Sat 10–4

Another of Oak Bay's trendy consignment shops, this one stocks ladies' clothing sized 8 to 48. They carry this full range of sizes, plus lovely new jewellery. Most of the garments are high-end, fashionable and current styles. They also carry a modest assortment of consigned maternity wear, too. Your consigned goods are seen by appointment only.

Cheques

2ND ACT FASHIONS
Sooke: 7–6726 West Coast Rd (642-4301)
Hours: Tue–Sat 10–5

This shop in the Sooke Merchant Centre offers "clean, quality ladies fashions at prices you can afford." Indeed, we found their stock fashionable and their prices modest. They insist that your consigned goods be current and very clean, but you can show them by dropping in any time they're open.

Cheques, credit cards

SHANK'S SADDLERY (consignments)—See Recreation

STILL LIFE—See Vintage

SUPER CHANCE DISCOUNT (consignment linens, clothing)—
See Bedding

TIME FOR A CHANGE CONSIGNMENTS
1541 Fort St (592-1419)
Hours: Tue–Fri 10–4:30; Sat 10–5

Donna, the owner, prefers to see your consigned garments only Tuesday to Friday, but appointments are not required. She carries men's and women's sportswear, plus purses, jewellery, shoes, hats and even some small housewares.

Cheques

TWICE AS NICE CONSIGNMENT BOUTIQUE
Colwood: 684 Granderson (478-1173)
Hours: Mon–Sat 10–5

Ladies' upscale clothing is the attraction here, with stock ranging—according to owner Dana—"from bathing suits to blue jeans to dresses." The emphasis caters to a youthful clientele. Your consignment may be seen or dropped off (if she's busy) any time during operating hours, and if she can't price it then, she'll call you back with her suggested selling prices.

Cheques, Visa only

TWICE-AROUND FASHIONS SHOP
1029 Cook St (383-3123)
Hours: Mon–Fri 10:30–5:30; Sat 10:30–5

A basic consignment shop with stylish women's clothing and accessories; the owners ask only that your garments are up-to-date, clean and in good condition. Consigned items are viewed Wednesday to Friday from 10:30 am to 4 pm.

Cheques

W.I.N. THRIFT STORE
1803 Cook St (389-2203)
Hours: Mon–Sat 10–5

"Thrift Store?" If you just wandered by, you'd swear it was a fancy boutique. Among the offerings are high quality antiques, clothing, excellent boots in prime condition (we spotted a pair of women's Frye boots in perfect shape last time) and really lovely women's fashions. A friend of ours bought an entire business suit there for only $5. (In truth, this entry should have appeared in our thrift store section, since all items are taken in by donation to benefit women and children in Transition House—W.I.N. stands for Women In Need—but we wanted to bring it to your attention, so we put it here instead.) Periodically, the shop runs a one-day "bag" sale, during which you can purchase a shopping bag in the store for $10 and fill it to the brim with any clothing that will fit inside. They'll usually discount housewares, linens, toys, books, shoes, records and accessories by 50%. We promise: This is not your standard thrift store.

Cheques

MATERNITY & CHILDREN'S WEAR

ABRA-KID-ABRA
2024 Oak Bay Ave (595-1613)
Hours: Mon–Sat 9:30–5

Everyone mentions Abra-Kid-Abra when you ask about children's clothing; it's one of the nicest consignment shops around. They also carry a line of their own new clothing and hats, and sell some cottage-industry garments. You can rent most kid equipment (i.e. high chairs), and there's a three-month cradle rental program. (There's always something sale priced, too.) They are always looking for clean consignment items, especially toys. You can drop your own consigned goods off anytime during open hours, but you'll just get a receipt and a call-back about pricing.

Credit cards

CLOWNING AROUND
2666 Quadra St (383-1122)
Hours: Mon–Sat 9:30–5

Consigned maternity wear is devilishly hard to find, but this shop has a good assortment, plus a nice line of new maternity duds. On the whole, it's women's wear and children's consignment, nicely arranged and in good condition. Your cast-offs (in clean condition, please) are accepted anytime during open hours, but for the next season only. (For example, they start accepting winter items in August.) Children's sizes range from infant to 14, and there's a full range of women's sizes. Toys and nursery equipment is always in demand.

Cheques, Credit cards

DESIGNER CONSIGNOR—See Consignment

FRUGAL FASHIONS—See Consignment

KIDDIN' AROUND
Sidney: 3–2372 Beacon Ave (656-1041)
Hours: Mon–Sat 10–5

Quality new and consigned children's clothing and accessories are the focus here, with togs available in a size 0-14 range; there are also nursery rentals and an exclusive line of locally made clothing by Jumping Jacks for Kids. Your consigned goods may be dropped off any time (they'll call you with prices in about a week), and all they ask is that items are in-season, clean and in good repair.

Cheques, Credit cards

KIDDO'S CONSIGNMENT FOR KIDS
Cedar Hill Mall, 103–1551 Cedar Hill X Rd (721-2330)
Hours: Mon–Sat 9:30–5

Kids' clothing, toys, books, bedding, shoes and boots are found here in great abundance. Consignment is accepted any time; they'll contact you to come and pick up items they don't want and check the prices they've set for your items. On your consignment sheet when you return, all items are listed, plus your contract expiry date. Return again on your expiry date, and your cheque and any unsold items await you. the split is the usual 50-50, and items are kept on sale for 60 days. Our friend, Helen Pearce, rates them as "great" and adds that Kiddo's has a good collection of toys and baby buggies. Find them behind McDonalds. Free underground parking at the mall.

Cheques

KIDS ONLY CLOTHING CLUB—See Factory Outlets

KIDSTUFF
688 Goldstream Ave (474-5040)
Hours: Mon–Sat 10–5

Here we found children's new and quality consignment clothing and accessories in a full size range. They always seek good-quality toys (a hint: Bag up puzzle pieces and make sure all toy parts are included for quicker resale), and they prefer to see kids' fashions in-season. Consignment viewing from 10 to 4 only. Another favorite of our friend Helen Pearce, who points out that they have "an interesting way of discounting items after three months—for super bargains!"

Credit cards

MOM'S CLOSET MATERNITY
827 Rock Heights Ave (388-0888)
Hours: Daily 9:30–9:30—by appointment only

This home-based business offers lots of sewing, plus consignment goods like dresses, new samples, business clothing and casual attire. Everything is top quality. Though they do sell outright, the main emphasis is on rental of maternity wear on a $50/month basis. (A formal maternity frock might cost $20 to rent for an evening.) Book an appointment by calling Heather at the number above.

Cheques, Credit cards

NARNIA WEAR—See Factory Outlets

NICE TWICE CONSIGNMENT SHOP
Colwood: 110–2244 Sooke Rd (478-9421)
Hours: Mon–Th & Sat 10–5; Fri 10–6

Among the typical consignment-store stock here are baby furnishings, buggies, toys and good quality clothing. They also take stylish men's and women's attire, plus small appliances. Says the owner, "If we've got room for it and it's in good condition, we'll take it." However, they see your consigned items only from 10 to 2 weekdays.

Cheques, Credit cards

NINOS FOR KIDS
104 – 1841 Oak Bay Ave (598-5118)
Hours: Mon–Sat 10–5:30; Sun noon–4

They prefer natural fibres (denim sells well), so it's no surprise that their stock is fresh and clean and of better quality than most. Kids' clothing is bought outright, and they also carry furniture, books and toys. Lesley the owner, will see incoming goods between noon and 1 or 5 to 5:30 on Wednesdays or Thursdays. (This is where we sell our outgrown items, by the way.)

Cheques, Credit cards

PANDORA'S CLOSET—**See Consignment**

WOW WALL TO WALL KIDS—**See Factory Outlets**

MEN'S DISCOUNT CLOTHING & CONSIGNMENT

ELLEY'S LEATHER—**See Factory Outlets**

FRUGAL FASHIONS—**See Consignment**

HOUSE OF SAVOY—Vintage

THE LEATHER RANCH—**See Factory Outlets**

MOORE'S THE SUIT PEOPLE
716 Johnson St (380-9334)
Hours: Mon–Wed & Sat 9:30–5:30; Th & Fri 9:30–9

Traditionally a great place for men's suit bargains, Moore's offers periodic "savings events," when their already low prices are slashed even further. (A recent sale had men's wool blend sportcoats reduced to $100 from $165.) Moore's claims to sell more sportcoats than anyone else in Canada—and no wonder: There's a huge size range—including stock for big and tall men—and many weights of different fabrics, many of them English blends and wools. The trench coats are a good deal, too, ranging in price from about $60 to $100 in many styles and colours. Free pant-hemming while you wait.

Cheques, Credit cards

MYSTIC LANE SHIRT CO—**See Factory Outlets**

NICE TWICE CONSIGNMENT SHOP—**See Maternity & Children's Wear**

OUT OF THE BLUE SPORTSWEAR—**See Factory Outlets**

SAVE ON SHIRTS—**See Factory Outlets**

VALHALLA OUTFITTERS—**See Factory Outlets**

ALTERNATE CLOTHING, HAND-DYED & CUSTOM CLOTHES

COMMAND POST OF MILITARIA
578 Yates St (383-4421)
Hours: Mon–Sat 10–5:30

The perfect place to find military items, Canadian, British and German war "souvenirs", war medals and cap badges from both world wars. The Command Post offers museum-quality framing and medal mounting and professional appraisals (they'll even make house calls). They are always seeking to buy Canadian air-force flying equipment (parachutes, rafts, Mae Wests, leather flying hats) and old uniforms, badges and headgear from law enforcement agencies.

Cheques, Credit cards

THE COSTUME SHOP AT LANGHAM COURT THEATRE
805 Langham Ct (384-2025)
Hours: Wed noon–5; Sat 10–2 only

Operating only two days a week, this rental outlet offers bargain prices on costumes for murder mysteries, masquerades and fancy dress balls. Ask for the manager, Jill, when you call to inquire.

Cheques

GLOBAL VILLAGE STORE
535 Pandora St (380-1530)
Hours: Mon–Sat 10–5

Volunteer-run and non-profit, the Global Village Store supports Third World co-ops, with most of the money raised going directly to the artisans who crafted the items. Among the stock are baskets, batiks, tie-dye goods and ornately embroidered vests, all at low prices. Self-described as "an alternative giftshop", they are precisely that, with products arriving daily from around the globe. They get batiks from a small group of widows in Calcutta, *arpilleras* from a women's workshop in Santiago and dolls from artisans in Nairobi. Among the groups they've aided are a Mennonite Central Committee project in Vietnam, a group of Mothers of the Disappeared in Guatemala and *Atelier des Cartes Postales,* a group of street boys in Rwanda who make unique greeting cards from banana leaves. These are gifts you can truly feel good about giving.

Cash only

THE GUATEMALAN SHOP
Market Square, 45–560 Johnson St. (386-2922)
Hours: Mon–Sat 10–6; Sun 11–6

Please see entry for RAINBOW MAYA SHOP (below), as both shops are run by the same people, with similar stock.

Credit cards

HEART'S CONTENT
18 Fan Tan Alley (380-1234)
Hours: Daily 11–5:30

This tiny shop features innovative and original hand-made garments which our tipster, the Empress Hotel's Deirdre Campbell, describes as "definitely alternative"—pretty much everything is one of a kind, and modestly priced, too.

Cheques, Credit cards

JOHN'S MILITARY SURPLUS
704 View St (360-2772)
Hours: Mon–Sat 9:30–5:30

There's a huge assortment of backpacks, totes, canteens, funky map bags, camouflage and army jackets, alongside serviceable (yet inexpensive) tents, camp cooking gear, sleeping bags, T-shirts, thick, practical socks, long underwear (tops or bottoms only $9.95) and cotton rags for only 50 cents for a giant bagful. A large panel of camouflage parachute material can be had for only $4. Everything for the grunge look.

Cheques, Credit cards

LITTLE TIBET SHOP
Address unavailable (381-5123)
Hours: Call for details

Formerly a well-known local "secret" in Fantan Alley, Bente Rehm's little shop closed last May so she could turn her fulltime efforts to other means of raising funds for needy Tibetan refugees. Now, she markets a line of fundraising greeting cards (wholesale and distributor inquiries welcome at the number above), and also sells some imported items on a direct-to-consumer basis.

Cheques

OFF THE CUFF
587 Johnson St (386-2221)
Hours: Mon–Sat 11:30–5:30; Sun (summer only)—phone for hours

This is the closest thing in town to to an authentic '60s head shop. (You do remember the '60s, don't you?) There's "tree-free" hemp paper from Ecosource, hemp fabric ("10 times stronger than cotton," goes the claim), a free bulletin board inside the door for messages ("Shotgun: See you at 4 if you got help. Fever and Jasmine"), and lots of biker paraphernalia—like ankle and handcuffs, lots of leather and medallions galore. We also saw a great deal of cannabis stuff and a sign offering hair-wraps for $1 an inch (cheap, considering the time involved). Music is deafening. Mind the sign saying "Do Not Touch Skulls—ask for assistance".

Credit cards

POLAR COW IMPORTS
105–3 Fan Tan Alley (388-7557)
Hours: Mon–Sat 10:30–5:30; Sun 11:30–4:30

"Definitely the Fringe" is the motto here, which seems about right for this alternative source for clothing and accouterments from India and Nepal. Friendly, happy sales people steeped in a haze of incense.

Cheques, Credit cards

PURPLE LAGOON CLOTHING
1284E Gladstone Ave (480-1192)
Hours: Tue–Sun noon–5; see text

Their credo is "Apparel on the Fringe"—but that fringe must be getting crowded by now. Anyway, they not only stock a wide selection of inexpensive, funky and unusual clothing and accessories, but they offer free incense to anyone who requests it. Just moving around the corner from their previous Fernwood Ave. address as we went to press, this operation was to be joining forces with Shazam (see below), with plans for "flexible" hours, so it would be best to call ahead.

Cheques

RAINBOW MAYA SHOP
Market Square, 45–560 Johnson St (384-2759)
Hours: Mon–Sat 10–6; Sun 11–6

We love this place and its sister operation just a few doors away in Market Square's lower courtyard. Prices are among the lowest in town for jewellery, souvenirs, gifts, ethnic clothing, Mexican hot spices and lovely blown glass inported from Latin America. They also carry inexpensive ponchos, woven clothing, colourful skirts, bright shirts and shorts.

Credit cards

SHAZAM IMPORTS
1284E Gladstone Ave (389-0713)
Hours: Tue–Th 11:30–5:30; Fri & Sat 12:30–6:30; Sun 1–4

We enjoy the lively alternative fashions assembled here by owner

Terrie Woods—very funky styles, particularly the great selection of men's ties. Love those gorgeous woven backpacks, too.

Cheques

STILL LIFE—See Vintage

THE WILDLIFE STORE
102 – 561 Johnson St (388-3560)
Hours: Mon–Sat 10:30–6; Sun noon–5

WINGS WILDLIFE NATURE BOUTIQUE
100 – 3170 Tillicum Rd (388-4264)
Hours: Mon, Tue & Sat 9:30–5:30; Wed–Fri 9:30–9; Sun noon–5

Both of the locations above are run by the same people. Everything in these shops is nature-themed: sweatshirts, pillows, bags, T-shirts, toy animals, cloth globes, novelties and jewellery. All stock is surprisingly inexpensive.

Credit cards

VINTAGE, FORMAL & BRIDAL WEAR

ANGELA FASHIONS
883 Fort St (480-0114)
Hours: Mon–Sat 10–5; Sun by appointment only

The only place in Victoria we found that will consign and resell bridal gowns. Angela also rents bride's wear, graduation dresses and formal gowns.

Cheques

HOUSE OF SAVOY
1869 Oak Bay Ave (598-3555)
Hours: Mon–Sat 10:30–5

Specializes in designer labels in both mens- and ladies wear, new, used and vintage clothing and jewellery. Consignments accepted daily.

Cheques

MAMA LOU'S VINTAGE CLOTHING
517 Yates St (380-0303)
Hours: Mon–Sat 11–6; Sun noon–5

Probably Victoria's best-known vintage clothing store, Mama Lou's also claims to have the city's largest selection of 501 jeans—and at bargain prices starting at $29.99. Jeans are "vintage" too, of course, and have been "chosen for their softness, worn spots, stress lines and fading." These qualities, they emphasize, "can only be achieved by years of washing. The look is authentic, lived-in classic denim."

Cheques, Credit cards

THE OLD VOGUE SHOP
950 Fort St (380-7751)
Hours: Mon–Sat 10–5:30; Sun call ahead

Vintage clothing is bought and sold here, and some items—those not bought outright—are taken in on consignment.

Cheques, Credit cards

RETREADS
Address not available (381-5000)
Hours: Anytime (machine takes calls during off-hours)

Margo Biggs had a wonderful clothing "recycling" business on Johnson Street until last April, but now she has even redesigned her business. Primarily, she offers inexpensive alterations, custom redesigning (in keeping with the vintage look of your out-worn duds), and she excels at creative patching, creating waist-coats/tails from suit jackets, replacing sleeves and so on, all at modest prices. Her other skill is pattern-drafting, and she will machine-hem a skirt for $6. Call any time for an appointment.

Cheques

SECOND HAND ROSE'S
101 – 561 Johnson St (386-3440)
Hours: Mon–Sat 10:30–5:30; Sun 1–5

Men's and ladies' consigned goods are taken and sold here, as well as locally designed jewellery, all at low prices. Local music and art are showcased in the store.

Credit cards

STILL LIFE

551 Johnson St (385-5655; fax: 380-5005

Hours: Mon–Sat 10:30–6; Sun noon–5

Self-described as "classic clothing", which in this case seems to encompass a great deal, Still Life sells new, vintage and charming consigned clothing (and alternative wear), primarily for women. They buy, sell and consign, and there's a bargain barrel at the front door.

Credit cards, InterAc

JEWELLERY, BEADS & FINDINGS

BEADWORLD

63 – 560 Johnson St (386-5534; fax: 360-2323)

Hours: Mon–Sat 9:30–6; Sun 11:30–5

One of our favourite destinations for just plain browsing, Beadworld makes shopping for beads and findings easy: You pick up a tray when you enter the store and drop your selections into separate compartments in the tray. The benefit of shopping in a store like this one is that you'll save money by assembling jewellery yourself, and the result is a truly one-of-a-kind creation. Their stock is enormous. Get home and realize you forgot to buy something? No problem: Beadworld will mail-order anything from their regular stock worldwide. Postal code is V8W 3C6.

Cheques, Credit cards

CITIZEN TIME & GOLD

723 Johnson St (388-4735)

Hours: Mon–Sat 9:30–5; Sun noon–5

Their Boxing Day sale features up to 40% off on watches like Seiko, Pulsar, Bulova, Citizen and even the top-of-the-line Movado, but the best bargain aspect of this place is that they accept trade-ins and offer instant service on battery replacement. There are more than 900 watches in stock at any given time.

Credit cards

ESQ. TRADING LTD
897 Esquimalt Rd (388-6542)
Hours: Mon–Sat 10–6; Sun noon–6

This family-run business (owners are Ed and Sarah Scott) is basically a pawnbroker: They buy, sell, trade and offer both custom jewellery and appraisals.

Credit cards

ETHOS
574 Johnson St (382-2131)
Hours: Mon–Th 11–5; Fri & Sat 10–5:30; Sun noon–4

Tucked in among a vast array of exotic apparel from around the world is a wondrous display of unique and funky jewellery. There are seasonal clearances and a regular section of sale items at 40% off.

Credit cards

JAYLYN JEWELLERS
Sidney: 2510 Bevan Ave (656-5556)
Hours: Tue–Sat 10–5

This is virtually a "factory-direct" store, because owner Jerome Reilander manufactures 90% of its fine jewellery on-site. "We can make jewellery to people's specifications and for a very reasonable price," says Jerome, "because we're not paying someone else to do it."

Credit cards

JEWELLATIONS
543 Johnson St (383-3250)
Hours: Mon–Sat 10–5:30; Sun noon–5

This make-your-own-accessory shop offers workshops and do-it-yourself materials (including hard-to-find jewellery books) for both the amateur crafter and the accomplished jewellery maker.

They stock beads and findings from around the globe, semi-precious stones, amber, ceramic, crystals, bone, horn and rare and ethnic beads, among many others; there's lots of locally made jewellery at prices you would expect to pay at the weekend market on Saltspring Island (artisan-direct, that is). They also teach an advanced class in Fimo millefiore technique, which is very popular; the $30 fee includes 6 blocks of Fimo clay.

Cheques, Credit cards, InterAc

STUDIO GLASS (glass earrings)—See Window Coverings

SHOES, FOOTWEAR & ACCESSORIES

FAWCETT SHOE REPAIRS
Sidney: 9767 4th St (655-4121)
Hours: Mon–Fri 9–5:30; Sat 9–4

Inexpensive repairs on boots and shoes—even runners. They also supply boat-top repairs, and suppies for do-it-yourselfers. They apply those durable Topy soles inexpensively and sell a small assortment of shoes at 25–60% off retail.

Cheques

THE ISLAND SHOE PLACE
2215 Oak Bay Ave (595-1144)
Hours: Mon–Sat 9–5:30

Sidney: 2378 Beacon Ave (656-5822)
Hours: Tue–Sat 9:30–5:30

The highlight here is the periodic "shoe rack" sales on Naturalizers.

Credit cards

OLDE TOWNE SHOE REPAIR
605 Johnson St (386-8333)
Hours: Mon–Fri 9–5:30

Expert repairs on Dr. Martens, Rockports and Birkenstocks bring repeat customers back to this downtown repair shop.

Cheques

SHOE STRINGS
1616 Cedar Hill X Rd (721-4577)
3082 Blanshard St (389-0667)
Hours: Mon–Wed & Sat 10–5:30; Th & Fr 10–9, Sun noon–5 (both)
119 – Tillicum Mall (381-4555)
Hours: Mon, Tue & Sat 10–5:30; Wed–Fri 10–9; Sun noon–5

This well-known B.C. discounter offers reduced prices on such brand names as Reebok, Nike, Brooks, Avia, Puma, Converse and Fila. They carry skates from Bauer, bodywear by Attivo and Heavenly Bodies and T-shirts from Adidas, Waves and Wolverine, to name but a few. Sizes and styles may be limited during clear-out sales and in merchandise culled from manufacturers ends-of-lines and discontinued stock. Out-of-towners can call toll free at 1-800-663-5636.

Credit cards

STEVENSON'S SHOE CLINIC
714 Fort St (383-8615)
Hours: Mon–Fri 8–5:30; Sat 9–5

Over 17 styles of satin shoes are available—and can be custom dyed—on the premises. They also rebuild Rockports, Mephisto, Birkenstock, Clark, Timberland and Vasque and sell a wide range of stock as well.

Cheques, Credit cards

VOLUME SHOES
727 Yates St (388-4495)
Hours: Mon–Th & Sat 9:30–5:30; Fri 9:30–6; Sun noon–4

The focus here is on family footwear and accessories. We found fine leather cocktail-length (short) boots price-slashed from $135 to $60 and smart looking leather handbags reduced to $20 from $39.

Cheques, Credit cards

WALK WITH RONSONS
639 – 3147 Douglas St (380-6552)
Hours: Mon, Tue 9–5:30; Wed–Fri 9–9; Sat 9:30–5; Sun noon–5

1005 Broad St (380-6500)
Hours: Mon–Sat 9–5:30

Mayfair Shopping Centre, 3147 Douglas St (380-6552)
Hours: Mon, Tue & Sat 9:30–5:30; Wed–Fri 9:30–9; Sun noon–5

Ronsons is known for its vast selection of styles and sizes, particularly in comfortable walking shoes. Periodic sales bring their regular prices even lower—like their discontinued-styles sales, when more than 4,000 pairs of shoes (regularly priced to $120) clear out for $50. Out-of-towners can call 1-800-465-7463 to verify that their sizes are in stock.

Cheques, Credit cards

NOTES:

4. FOOD

According to Statistics Canada, the average B.C. family spent over 20% of its entire yearly expenditure on food in 1982. Since then, prices have risen steadily, and most incomes have barely kept pace with that increase. Victoria is still one of the most expensive cities in Canada in which to fill a grocery basket.

Never have B.C. consumers needed to be so price-conscious. We know that 392 million food discount coupons are distributed annually to entice us to buy this brand or that (fewer than 4% of the $70 million represented by coupons are ever redeemed). What this means is that our buying power is impressive, and local food wars indicate a strong appreciation of that power on the part of food merchants. By altering your buying habits, you should be able to save up to 30%. Therefore, if your monthly food budget is $400, you should be able to save about $120. Here are two pieces of advice:

• Learn to buy in large quantities, preferably by sharing bulk purchases with a co-op group or a few friends. Your best buys will be in quantity lots.
• Understand current prices to know when you are buying at bargain prices. Not all outlets sell everything for less than supermarkets, even at the discount "bag your own" places.

One other caution: Many wholesalers at factory outlets barely tolerate individual buyers. Many deal in multi-case lots or truckloads. Selling a few items disrupts their operations. Tread lightly in these situations. Insisting on special service or interfering with regular business could close some of these outlets to you, and to others like you who are interested in buying food for less. Please don't spoil a good situation for everyone.

As a bargain measure, consider home delivery of milk products. Please see our section on Produce, Eggs and Dairy Products for two sources—and you save the inconvenience of carting heavy milk cartons home.

SUPERMARKETS

Everyone we know complains about how expensive it is to shop for food in Victoria. Typically, food stores do not list their phone numbers in the directory, making it hard to shop around for, say, the best price on large sacks of sugar for jelly-making and canning. We agree that Victoria's grocery scene presents a challenge, but we've found that by scanning the weekly flyers for limited-time discounts (and acting promptly), we can usually stock up on specials—especially on staple foods. (It pays to own a chest freezer.) Flyers are almost always posted inside the market, and window signs advertising specials are updated weekly. Watch also for stores featuring "Everyday Low Prices" (known in the industry as "EDLP"), which usually indicate cheaper prices due to the store's ability to buy in volume. Here are some general guidelines about who stocks the best of the cheapest, and on what items:

BRENTWOOD TRU-VALUE FOOD CENTRE
Saanichton: Wallace Dr & West Saanich Rd (phone unavailable)
Hours: Daily 8 a.m.–9:30 p.m.

Low sale prices here on seafood, produce and some staple items. Everyday low prices (EDLP) on many others.

Cheques

FAIRWAY MARKETS
Canwest Mall, 2945 Jacklin Rd (phone unavailable)
Colwood Plaza, 1900 Sooke Rd (phone unavailable)
Hours: Mon–Sat 8–9; Sun 9–9 (Vanwest & Colwood)
Gorge Shopping Ctr, 2900 Tillcum Rd (phone unavailable)
Shelbourne Plaza, 3600 Shelbourne (phone unavailable)
Hours: Mon–Sat 8–10; Sun 9–9 (Gorge & Shelbourne)
Town & Country, 3600 bl. Douglas St (phone unavailable)
Hours: Mon–Sat 8–10; Sun 8–9

These businesses have been locally owned since 1963 and offer excellent weekly specials in a full range of grocery items. There's also an extensive bulk foods section.

Cheques

FOOD COUNTRY
230 Cook St (382-5213; fax: 382-2687)
Hours: Daily 8:30 a.m.–9 p.m.

Free delivery Tuesday to Saturday in their "trading area" enhances the deals at Food Country, which offers some of the best sale prices for produce we've seen. Garden stock is often sale-priced in season, too.

Cheques, Credit cards, InterAc

FOOD FORUM
Cordova Bay: 5124 Cordova Bay Rd (phone unavailable)
Oak Bay: 2585 Cadboro Bay Rd (phone unavailable)
Hours: Mon–Sat 9–9, Sun 10–6:30

You get 10% off everything (except tobacco, milk, butter and stamps) with a minimum $5 purchase, every Tuesday. Mondays, the deal is 10% off all fresh cut meats. They also offer weekly specials and an EDLP policy.

Cheques

GORDON HEAD FOOD MART
4343 Tyndall Ave (477-1414)
Hours: Mon–Sat 9–10; Sun 9–9:30

See Lewis Low Cost listing (below) for details.

Cheques

HILLSIDE MARKET
Hillside Mall, 1644 Hillside Ave (592-0101)
Hours: Mon–Fri 9:30–9; Sat 9:30–5:30; Sun 11–5

This market-in-a-mall offers a variety of specialty foods and exotic imports from a number of independent vendors under one roof. Prices are often yuppie-calibre, but each shopping area in the market offers weekly specials, so something's always on sale. Choose from pasta, the Swedish Bakery (fabulous bread and rolls), Turkey Specialties (the only store in the area that specializes in turkey), Logical Foods (see listing under Natural Foods), the Market Butcher (some say the best in town), Rising Star (another excellent bakery renowned for its cheesecakes—See listing under Bakery Goods) and everything from "Best of British" to Mexican to Chinese food to salad takeouts.

Cheques, Cash preferred

JUBILEE FOOD MARKET
1803 Fort St (595-1113)
Hours: Mon–Sat 8:30–8:30; Sun 9:30–8

See Lewis Low Cost listing (below) for details.

Cheques

LEWIS LOW COST FOOD & MEAT MARKET
289 Foul Bay Rd (phone unavailable)
Hours: Mon–Sat 9–9; Sun 10–7

Part of a Capital Regional District buying group of 12 stores, this one is typical in its offerings of weekly specials, particularly in the produce department. Others in the group are: Vic's Super Save (384-4513), Jubilee Food Market (595-1113), Casey Low Cost, Niagara Low Cost, Much More Foods & Video (360-2222), Willoway Low Cost, Gordon Head Food Mart (477-1414), V & J Super Low

Cost, Corona Low Cost, McRae Food Market (592-1731), Walls Food Market (595-5931), Cadboro Bay Low Cost, and Resthaven Store (656-1140) in Sidney.

Cheques

MCRAE FOOD MARKET
1652 McRae Ave (592-1731)
Hours: Daily 9–10

See Lewis Low Cost listing (above) for details.

Cheques

MR GROCER
1153 Esquimalt Rd (382-5515)
4440 West Saanich Rd (479-7112; fax; 479-5537)
Hours: Daily 8 a.m.–11 p.m.

We've seen prices such as a 5-pound bag of grapefruit or the same weight in carrots, each for 99 cents, here. Again, check flyers and in-store promotion for the best values.

Cheques

MUCH MORE FOODS & VIDEO
1120 Hillside Ave (360-2222)
Hours: Mon–Sat 9–9; Sun 10–9

See Lewis Lost Cost listing (above) for details.

Cheques

OXFORD FOODS
271 Cook St (phone unavailable)
Hours: Mon–Fri 9–9; Sat 9–6; Sun 10–6

Though this is a relatively small store, Oxford still maintains a solid policy of weekly specials. Among the bargains are excellent prices on fresh or smoked meats.

Cheques

QUADRA GROCERY—See RED MANGO/QUADRA GROCERY under Restaurants

RESTHAVEN STORE
Sidney: 10425 Resthaven Dr (656-1140)
Hours: Daily 8–9

Owner David Scott joins his cronies in the Core-Mark buying group (see Lewis Low Cost listing, above) to bring super values to his customers through volume buying. Specials are announced regularly in community newspapers and in the store.

Cheques, Cash preferred

SAVE-ON FOODS & DRUGS
Saanich: 3510 Blanshard St (384- 3311)
Hours: Daily 8 a.m.–midnight

Almost everyone we polled in Victoria for this book made some mention of the bargains at Save-On Foods. In our personal experience, however, we've sometimes found that great deals and not-so-great prices may be side-by-side, so we advise you to know your prices. Weekly sales are announced via flyers in the local papers and copies are available in the store. Look for specials on electronics (and video games), produce, meats, gardening gear and nursery stock, kitchen wear (an excellent series recently offered stainless steel cookware at low, low prices) and, of course, the great bulk foods section. Service is excellent, and there are even free, informative store tours (called "Shop Smart Tours") for groups; enquire at the customer service desk. Books and magazines are routinely discounted by 10% at the cash register. A notice board area near the entrance offers local person-to-person bargains.

Cheques, Credit cards

SIDNEY SUPER FOODS
Sidney: 2531 Beacon Ave (phone unavailable)
Hours: Mon–Wed & Sat 8:15–6:30; Th & Fri 8:15–9; Sun 9–6

This is another one to watch for weekly specials. Though we find the everyday prices a little higher than in Victoria proper, there can be good values on dairy products and produce.

Cheques

STADACONA FOOD MART
1563 Pandora Ave (598-3168)
Hours: Mon–Sat 9–9; Sun 10–7

Specials include 2-for-1 video rentals and low prices on produce specials, as various local items come into season.

Cheques, Cash preferred

THRIFTY FOODS
Customer service (for all): 544-1234
1590 Fairfield Rd
3995 Quadra St
475 Simcoe St
Broadmead Village, 777 Royal Oak Dr
Sidney: 9810 7th St
Hours: Daily, 8 a.m.–10 p.m.

Colwood: 1860 Island Hwy
Mill Bay: 2720 Mill Bay Rd
Hours: Daily, 8 a.m.–9 p.m.

These locally owned stores advertise vast numbers of weekly specials in regional newspapers, with excellent savings available to the careful shopper. Discounts are offered on the full range of grocery products, from meat and seafood to staple items, produce and baked goods. Flyer prices are in effect from Wednesday to the following Tuesday. For long-distance inquiries, call toll free, 1-800-667-8280.

Cheques

WALLS FOOD MARKET
1279 Bay St (595-5931)
Hours: Mon–Sat 9–9; Sun 11–9

See Lewis Low Cost listing (above) for details.

Cheques

WELLBURN'S FINE FOODS (MARKET)
1058 Pandora Ave (384-3543)
Hours: Mon–Sat 9 a.m.–10 p.m.; Sun 10–10

This is probably our favourite discount grocery store: Ample parking at the side, late hours daily, and serious discounts on many products every week. We eschew the soft drinks (which are almost always cheaper at nearby London Drugs), but return regularly for the fresh bread and baked goods, excellent deals on meat and dairy, and the friendly cashiers, always helpful and smiling. Again, check weekly advertised specials.

Credit cards

BAKERY GOODS

BENNY'S BAGELS
132–560 Johnson St (384-3441)
112–1644 Hillside Ave (598-4353)
Hours: Mon–Sat 7–7; Sun 10–7

Victoria is where bagelmeisters Michael Hallatt and Colin Gareau started their business, and Benny's is still the best place in town for fresh bagels, though hardly the 24-hour hip hangout the the mainland store has become. Prices are competitive, and day-old bagels (perfect for slicing thin and turning into bagel crisps in the oven) are discounted.

Cash only

BUNS MASTER BAKERY
751 Vanalman Ave (727-6577)
Big Barn Market, 1286 McKenzie Ave (477-1663)
Langford: 672 Granderson Rd (474-3441)
Oak Bay: 2579 Cadboro Bay Rd (592-3231)
Sidney: 101–2376 Bevan Ave 655-3633
Hours: Mon–Sat 9:30–6; Sun 10–5

Buns Master offers fresh bread daily at factory prices. Good selection is available, and daily (or weekly) specials are offered in addition to regular discounts. Included in the ever-expanding stock are various kinds of bread, dozens of types of buns (braided, dinner rolls, hot dog and hamburger buns, etc.) as well as finish-it-yourself pizza crusts, foccacia, cinnamon buns, doughnuts, fresh-baked pies, muffins, cookies and more. Seniors get a 10% discount Wednesdays. Watch community newspapers for coupons announcing spotlight specials.

Cheques

CHERRY BLOSSOM DESSERTS
2000 Douglas St (381-4488, 384-9922)
Hours: Mon–Fri 8–5, Sat 9–4

A variety of cheesecakes and tortes are baked on site here. While per-slice prices are about par with restaurant costs, you'll save if you buy an entire cake for entertaining. Prices for 2-1/2 lb tortes range from $23.50 to $25 for the 9-inch size (pre-cut into 14 pieces and pre-papered between cuts), to 10-inch cheesecakes (weighs about 4 pounds): Plain $21; liquor $26; fruit $22.50; and flavoured $24.75. Cheesecakes also serve 14 and are pre-papered for ease of serving. These prices save you 30–50% off restaurant retail.

Cheques

JOHN'S PLACE BAKERY
2405 Douglas St (386-1233)
Hours: Tue–Sat 9:30–5:30

John's Place Bakery claims to make the best cheesecake in town. They also bake fresh bread daily, sell frozen foccacia dough (a good value), homemade pies, deluxe muffins and gourmet cookies, all at low prices.

Cheques, Credit cards

MOUNT ROYAL BAGEL FACTORY
Grant St at Cook St, see text (380-3588)
Hours: Tue–Sat 8–6; Sun 8–4

Though the mailing address is #6, 1115 North Park, the store actually faces toward Grant St, just north of Cook. For those who seek authentic Montreal-style bagels (a little more dense and chewy than New York- or Toronto-style), this is the place, the brainchild of two ex-Montreal guitarists, Elliott Silverman and Mark Workman, who went into business because they were frustrated by not being able to find Montreal bagels in Victoria. Pat

Donovan, a jazz bass player also originally from Montreal, is their weekend baker. Discounts are available on bulk orders.

Cash only

OAK BAY VILLAGE BAKERY & DELI

2217 Oak Bay Ave (598-1911)

Hours: Mon–Fri 6:30 a.m.–5:30; Sat 6:30–5

We found prices here reflected about 20% savings across the board over other retail bake shops. There are eccles cakes, cinnamon buns and Dutch apple turnovers for 93 cents, hot cross buns for $1.75 per half dozen, butter tart squares (handy for freezing) at 84 cents, big slabs of strudel for $7.95, regular butter tarts at 85 cents apiece, and every kind of bread, all hot and fresh from the oven. Cheery staff.

Credit cards

OLD ENGLISH PIE SHOP

416 Craigflower Rd (386-4633)

Hours: Mon–Fri 3 a.m.–2 p.m. (really)

Owner Hilda Mason starts work in the wee hours to provide some serious baking for the Vic West community. Here, among the huge international doll collection and the Chuck-and-Di memorabilia, Hilda sells almost all kinds of meat pies: Steak & mushroom, steak & kidney, chicken pot pie, cornish pasty and bacon, egg & tomato. There's also spinach & fettucine, mushroom quiche and salmon & spinach turnovers. Pies, at $2.75 each, can be mixed-and-matched with others for a bargain price of $2.25 each on orders of six or more. In addition, Hilda makes butter tarts, carrot cake, date squares, giant baked sticky-buns, wondrous bran muffins and a to-die-for lemon meringue pie ($1.50 a slice or $8 for the whole pie).

Cash only

RISING STAR WHOLE FOODS BAKERY

1320 Broad St (386-2534)

Hours: Mon–Fri 7:30–5:30; Sat 8:30–4:30

118 – 1670 Hillside Ave (598-3515)

Hours: Mon, Tue & Sat 9:30–5:30; Wed–Fri 9:30–9;
Sun 11–5:30

What started almost two decades ago as a small co-op bakery in Vic West (specializing in whole grain baking) is now a major bakery and espresso bar, with the focus still on healthy foods. Rising Star also sells light lunches, croissants, pastries, vegetarian fare and wonderful cheesecakes. Wholesale prices are available on bulk purchases.

Cheques

ROBERTSHAW SPECIALTY PIES
2865 Foul Bay Rd (592-3314)
Hours: Mon–Sat 8–6

Meat pies are available here in steak, chicken, and steak & kidney for $2.55 each. Discounts are available for bulk orders. Fruit pies come in apple, strawberry, rhubarb, loganberry, blueberry and marianberry (a blackberry-loganberry cross), each for $3.99.

Cheques, Cash preferred

BEVERAGES

In this section, you'll discover great sources for discount tea and coffee (and accoutrements important in brewing these beverages). Also, new to Victoria and spreading rapidly is a twist on the beverage business: The U-brew. Generally speaking, these places not only afford discriminating beer or wine drinkers the option to choose from a vast array of finished beverages, but also gain the satisfaction of making it themselves. Best of all, you'll enjoy the results for at least half the cost of buying it at liquor stores. Some places sell the equipment necessary to make your own at home; others allow you to brew on their premises and return to bottle your booty.

AVALON COTTAGE
1157 Newport Ave (595-7770)
Hours: Tue–Sat 9:30–5:30

Avalon Cottage operates a "hop-line" (number above) to answer questions on brewing, and it sells from a vast inventory of European juices and concentrates and many recipes for beers and ales. Plenty of ancillary supplies for your home brewing.

Cheques, Credit cards

CAIRO COFFEE MERCHANTS
1609 Douglas St (384-6321)
Hours: Mon–Fri 7–5:30; Sat & Sun 9–5

DESIGNER BEANS
744 Fort St (386-3937)
Hours: Mon–Sat 9–5:30

Organic Guatemalan coffee is sold here for $10.75 for 400 grams. There's a clearance section of china and kitchenware, and the "cup of the hour" is brewed and sold for only 75 cents, a serious bargain price these days. For take-out, there's hot chocolate or espresso at $1, cappuccino at $1.75 and tea for 75 cents, all below the standard prices in local coffee shops.

Cash only

FERMENTHAUS
3200 Quadra St (386-1023)
Hours: Tue–Fri 11–5:30; Sat 11–5

This wine, beer and liquor supplies outlet sells ingredients and equipment for use at home.

Credit Cards, only for Victoria-area customers

HAMILTON HOPS & GRAPES
464A Burnside Rd East (388-4511)
Hours: Mon–Fri 10–5:30; Sat 10–5

Longtime pals and Victoria residents Marilyn Wargo and Cary Corbeil frequent these wine and beer suppliers, who they say are "known for their friendly and helpful service" and low prices.

Cheques, Credit cards

HOBBY BEER & WINES
1302 Finlayson St (382-2739)
Hours: Mon–Sat 10–6

You'll find wine kits, Cooper's malt extracts and lots of books on wine and beer making. Hobby also carries Pop Shoppe discount ("no name") soft drinks. Ample parking alongside the building.

Credit cards

MURCHIE'S TEA & COFFEE—See Kitchen Equipment & China

PENINSULA U-BREW
Sidney: 207–2031 Malaview Ave (655-7121)
Hours: Mon–Sat 8–5:30

You'll find a complete line of home brewing products at Peninsula U-Brew, which is right across from Slegg Lumber. Owner Andy Miller oversees the preparation of your beer (more than 40 varieties) or wine (more than 60). Cost runs about $1 to $3.75 per bottle of wine and $8 per case of beer. Processing time takes about 4 to 6 weeks; you then return to bottle your wine and take it home. Andy claims that Peninsula's better wines compare with those selling at the liquor store for up to $14, so "it allows people to drink a good wine for a reasonable price."

Cheques, Credit cards

RISING STAR WHOLE FOODS BAKERY (espresso)—See Bakeries

SELF-HEAL HERBS (herbal teas)—See Drug Needs, Vitamins

SILK ROAD (herbal teas)—See Cosmetics

SOOKE U BREW
2044 Otter Point Rd (642-7787)
Hours: Tue & Wed noon–6, Th & Fri 11–7; Sat 10–4

This is an on-premise brewing facility where beer takes about two weeks to make and saves you that 50% off beer store prices as mentioned earlier. Lots of helpful, free advice.

Cheques

SUNFLOWER (beer and wine-making supplies)—See Natural Foods

WEST COAST BREW SHOP
Vic West: 155B Langford St (384-8484)
Hours: Tue–Fri noon–8; Sat 9–5

Another opportunity to brew your own on someone else's premises, West Coast guarantees premium, all-natural beer and wine, assisted by the expert advice of their brewmaster. Boasting a "unique partial mash", "custom-steam-heated brew kettles" and "superior counter-pressure bottling system," they've been in business as a family-owned and -operated business for five years, so they've obviously won a following. Again, expect savings of about 50% off retail. Free parking.

Cheques, Credit cards

WINE ART
1125 Haultain St (381-5332)
Hours: Tue–Fri 9:30–5:30; Sat 9–5

This is a source for supplies to brew beer or make wine in your home. Lots of instructional books and plenty of free advice. A good place to rent a wine press when your home vines need harvesting. Limited parking, shared by Haultain Fish & Chips.

Cheques, Credit cards

THE WINEMAKER
1736A Island Hwy (474-4405)
Hours: Tue–Th & Sat 10–5:30, Fri 10–7

If they don't answer the phone, they're "looking after their wine." Personalized service. Many wine kit choices.

Cheques, Credit cards

ZACHERY BEAN
749 View St (380-0515)
Hours: Mon–Sat 7–6

719 Yates St (480-1163)
Hours: Mon–Th 7–midnight; Fri & Sat 7–2a.m.; Sun 9–midnight

Sidney: 2505 Beacon Ave (655-3606)
Hours: Mon–Th 7–10; Fri & Sat 7–10:30; Sun 8–9

This locally owned and operated chain offers discounts regularly in community papers, such as: Bring in your theatre ticket and receive 20% off any purchase of your choice; or present the ad and receive two regular coffees for the price of one.

Cheques

ZANZIBAR
734 View St (383-3511)
Hours: Daily 9 a.m.–midnight

As with Zachery Bean, you can regularly take advantage of a 50 cents-off coupon in the community newspapers, reducing the cost of a latte to $1.50.

Cash only

CANDY & TREATS

THE ENGLISH SWEET SHOP
738 Yates St (382-3325)
Hours: Mon–Fri 9:30–5; Sat 10–5

This long, narrow shop is jam-packed with imported bulk candy of every stripe—licorice, toffee, wine gums, butterscotch, hard candies (like hard-to-find bulls' eyes) and milk chocolate bars that, coming from England, do taste different even though you may be familiar with the brand names. There's a selection of sugar-free chocolate and imported canned goods (mushy peas!), soft drinks and china (mugs, teapots and cups). Mail order service available. Postal code is V8W 1L4.

Credit cards

ROGERS' TUDOR SWEET SHOPPE
2228 Oak Bay Ave (598-2911)
Hours: Mon–Fri 9:30–5:30; Sun 11–5

Like at the English Sweet Shop on Yates, you'll find an array of imported hard candies and toffees here. Interestingly, for 50 cents each, you can buy miniatures of Rogers' famous creams—which aren't available at Rogers' Government St flagship store.

Credit cards

ETHNIC FOODS

B & V MARKET
3198 Quadra St (380-1455)
Hours: Daily 9–10

Victoria bargain maven Marilyn Wargo tipped us to this source, which she describes as "one of the only markets that sells East Indian foods."

Cash

CONTI DELICATESSEN
1223 Government St (383-9221)
Hours: Tue–Fri 9:30–5:30; Sat 8:30–4:30

What a great find: This narrow, little shop has a markdown table with a variety of food and non-food items all at 50% off, and otherwise sells all kinds of German comestibles at modest prices. We found an assortment of fine German sausage, a goodly selection of jams, herbal teas, choice espressos and chocolate, plus a number of European newspapers and magazines. A notice board at the door gives news from the Victoria Edelweiss Club.

Cash only

ITALIAN FOOD IMPORTS
1114 Blanshard St (385-7923)
Hours: Mon–Fri 9–5:30; Sat 9:30–5

Though there are a couple of red-check-tableclothed tables just inside the door, we think of this as more of a grocery than a cafe. On the shelves, there are large (economy-sized) jars of products you may indeed find elsewhere—but not at these prices: 680 ml of artichoke hearts, for example, at $4.55. Plenty of pasta in every conceivable shape, bottled and canned sauces, capers, herbs and spices, olive oils and balsamic vinegar. Delicious fresh olives and cheeses. Proud and helpful owners (from Venice) make you feel you've stepped into an Italian movie.

Mastercard

MARKS & SPENCER
114 Victoria Eaton Centre (386-6727)
Hours: Mon–Wed & Sat 9:30–5:30; Th & Fri 9:30–9;
Sun noon–5

If you're craving a taste of England—literally—the food department of "Marks & Sparks" is a must visit. It's on the basement level at the Eaton Centre and offers an amazing array of imported or licensed foodstuffs: Cookies, crackers, candy, beverages, canned vegetables and a frozen food section that runs the gamut of traditional English fare—shepherd's pie, fish and chips, bangers (as in mash) and so on. There are everyday sale items, but the discounts on candy and cakes after the big holidays (especially Christmas and Easter) are extraordinary; they're often packaged in attractive tins that are worth the price alone.

Credit cards

PHILIPPINE ORIENTAL GROCERIES & NOVELTIES
3185 Quadra St (386-6525)
Hours: Mon–Sat 10:30–5

Here's a good source for reasonably priced Asian spices and (low-quality) novelties and toys.

Cash only

NATURAL FOODS: GRAINS, SEEDS, CEREALS, SPICES & BULK FOOD

BABE'S HONEY FARM
Saanich: 334 Walton Pl (658-8319)
Hours: Mon–Sat 9–5; Sun 11–5

We were delighted to find this straight-from-the-farm source for honey, beeswax and bee pollen, because we've always liked the Babe's honey we've bought in local grocery stores. Everything is sold at low farm prices: $1.50/lb for honey, a small beeswax for 50 cents, otherwise $3.20/lb. If you have a real sweet tooth, 15 kg (33 lb) of honey is $49.50, plus $1 for the bucket deposit or bring your own container to fill there.

Cheques

LOGICAL FOODS
Hillside Market, 104–1670 Hillside Ave (595-4224)
Hours: Mon, Tues & Sat 9:30–5:30; Wed–Fri 9:30–9; Sun 11–5
University Heights Shopping Ctr, 7–3960 Shelbourne (721-4227)
Hours: Mon–Wed & Sat 9:30–5:30; Th & Fri 9:30–9; Sun noon–5

Look for weekly sales on Logical's healthy stock—everything from wild rice (regularly $6.49 lb, reduced to $4.79) to pitted baking dates ($1.99 lb, reduced to $1.29) to walnut crumbs (regularly $3.39 lb, marked down to $2.09) to dried apple rings (regularly $5.49 lb, down to $3.59) to flax seed (regularly 55 cents, reduced to 35). There are also sales (up to 25 per cent off) on selected body care products.

Cheques, Credit cards

NATURE'S FARE (natural foods)—**See Drug Needs & Vitamins**

THE NUTSHELL GROCERY
170–911 Yates St (383-4686)
Hours: Mon–Fri 10–6:30; Sat & Sun 10–6

This small but jam-packed bulk store opposite London Drugs is a chef's or baker's delight. (It's great, too, if you just have the munchies.) Recent prices: Thompson seedless raisins (23 cents/100g), organic Manitoba wild rice ($4.25/lb), medjool dates (93 cents/100g), organic B.C. apple juice ($3.99/1.9 litres). Limited free parking.

Cheques, Credit cards

ONE WORLD HEALTH FOODS
Broadmead Village, 777 Royal Oak Dr (727-2474)
Hours: Mon–Th 9:30–7; Fri 9:30–9; Sat 9:30–5:30; Sun 11–5:30

This full-service natural food store also sells vitamins and health supplements, such as evening primrose oil. Periodic sale prices are common—watch local papers for ads. They also regularly carry Rice Dream (non-dairy ice cream) and beverages like Santa Cruz natural, organic, sweet apple cider.

Cheques, Credit cards

PLOUGHSHARE
4649 West Saanich Rd (479-2322)
Hours: Daily 8–7

Here's a source for local fruits and vegetables, nuts, seeds, dried fruit, fresh cut flowers, dairy products, fresh baked goods, bulk foods and a plethora of organic products, all at low prices.

Cheques

SEED OF LIFE NATURAL FOODS
1316 Government St (382-4343)
Hours: Mon–Sat 9–5:30

This natural foods store dates back to 1977 and offers a host of allergy alternatives, such as rice beverages, egg replacers, gluten-free flours, cheese substitutes and more. They offer Studentsaver discounts, one hour of free parking (inquire in store) and bulk honey at $1.25/lb (bring your own containers). There's a display of "penny" candies, all more healthful versions than we remember from our youth.

Cheques, Credit cards

SUNFLOWER
Brentwood Bay: 7060 West Saanich Rd (652-1211)
Hours: Mon–Sat 9:30–5; Sun 11–5:30

This Brentwood Bay health-food outlet offers substantial discounts during its periodic sales: 10 per cent off packaged foods, 15 per cent off bulk foods, and 10 to 20 per cent off vitamin supplements. They also offer occasional discounts on already-low-priced beer and wine-making supplies.

Cheques, Credit cards

VITEWAY NATURAL FOODS
1019 Blanshard St (384-5677; fax: 384-9533)
Hours: Mon–Fri 9:30–7; Sat 11–5; Sun noon–5

This is unquestionably, as billed, "Victoria's Complete Health and Nutrition Centre." Organic is the byword here—everything from soup mixes, pasta, juices, breads, produce, honey, peanut butter, aromatherapy and essential oils, gluten-free and milk-free products, liquid amino acids, herbal remedies and PMS-relief aids. Champion juicers were $50 off recently (down to $269), and there were free nutritional consulations. A discount of 10% is offered on everything in the store on Sundays.

Credit cards

PRODUCE, EGGS AND DAIRY PRODUCTS

BIG BARN GARDEN CENTRE
1286 MacKenzie Ave (477-4435, 477-9495; fax: 477-0012)
Hours: Mon–Fri 8:30–8; Sat & Sun 8:30–6

This large supermarket offers really competitive weekly specials, plus superior produce and a burgeoning garden shop—one of the best stocked in town.

Cheques, Credit cards

ISLAND FARMS DAIRIES CO-OP ASSOCIATION
2220 Dowler Pl (260-5200; home service: 360-5211; fax: 384-5869)
Hours: Phones open Mon–Fri 8–5

Home delivery costs you nothing and saves you wear and tear on carrying heavy bottles and packages, but the deal here is in periodic sales offered only to home delivery clients. Deliveries are usually twice a week—precisely which days depending on where you live. All sizes of milk, plus glass and bulk plastic packs are available, and they deliver eggs, sour cream, bread and English muffins. In the summer, specialty items like freezer pops are added to the delivery line. You are invoiced twice a month and may pay by cheque.

Cheques

NATURE'S FARE (organic produce)—**See Drug Needs & Vitamins**

PLOUGHSHARE—**See Natural Foods**

RED BARN FARM MARKET
5550 West Saanich Rd (479-8349)
Hours: daily 7:30–6

Recommended to us by an Island seed wholesaler, Red Barn sells some of the freshest (and cheapest) produce around, and its plants and cut flowers are plentiful and low-cost. They have a huge produce section (mainly farm-fresh, organic) including (in season) nu-spuds, Macs, peaches, cabbage, berries, fresh peas (the best we've ever eaten) and farm-fresh eggs. Serve yourself from bins outside and in the store. Elsewhere in the store are Portuguese buns (3/99 cents), gourmet rainbow lollipops, mix and match candies, Michelle's natural 2-minute pasta, instant refried beans from flakes, fresh herbs, bulk foods, beans and spices and more. One of our favourite bargain spots.

Cheques

ROYAL OAK DAIRY
759 Vanalman Ave (479-5097)
Hours: Mon–Sat 9–6; Sun 10:30–5:30

A relative newcomer to the local food scene, Royal Oak has been running an aggressive ad campaign to get its products into Victoria grocery stores. Meanwhile, the savvy consumer can benefit from their home delivery—or shop directly at the dairy for bottled milk. You'll save 12% if you buy $40 worth of products; better still, you don't have to buy milk all at once to save—you can purchase a "milk buying card" for $40 and use it for purchases until your credit is used up.

Cheques

WILDLIFE CARVINGS (farm-fresh eggs)—**See Decorative Accents**

SEAFOOD

BAY SCALLOPS
Fisherman's Wharf (phone unavailable)
Hours: Catch-as-catch-can (see text)

We've only found the little sales shack open once on our excursions to Fisherman's Wharf at the foot of St. Lawrence St, but the bargains are there if you arrive when they're open. There's lots of fresh seafood, especially scallops, of course.

Cash only

FISHERMAN DIRECT FISH SALES
2581 Blackwood St (388-3474 or 383-5715)
Hours: 24-hour messages

Here's the place to buy seafood at fisherman-direct prices. They're usually out fishing, but call either number and leave word on the answering machine and they'll get back to you with what's fresh in the hold—and prices.

Cash preferred

LIVE CRAB
Fisherman's Wharf, Dock 6 (360-1943)
Hours: Fri, Sat, Sun—noon–4 or while stock lasts

Though the address of Fisherman's Wharf is St. Lawrence St, you'll find the wharf at the foot of Dallas Road near Laurel Point. The entrance is just past Erie St, and there's pay parking (be sure to put your 50 cents in the meter, for the parking commissioners watch the area carefully). The crab is fresh-caught just off Sooke or Sidney, and sells for $5 (small), $6 (medium), $7 (large). It's a family-run business. Their advice: "Boil the water and throw them in. When the water comes back to the boil, let them cook for 12 minutes." Said a regular customer about the crabs struggling to get out of their plastic bag:"They usually double-bag 'em. If you think they're fighting now, you should see them trying to jump out of the hot water!" A hint: Bring your own canvas bag lined with plastic, and use a large pot when you cook them at home.

Cash only

NOTES:

5. PERSONAL CARE

COSMETICS, PERFUMES, GROOMING & BEAUTY SUPPLIES

ARDMORE HARMONY HOUSE
Sidney: 9594 Ardmore Rd (656–1845)
Hours: phone ahead (home business)

This independent Shaklee distributor sells their full line of products. Also see Shaklee, below.

Cheques

AS NATURE INTENDED
3820 Gordon Head Rd (477–5334)
Hours: 24-hour machine

This independent Shaklee distributor sells their full line of products. Also see Shaklee, below.

Cheques

PERFECT SCENTS DISTRIBUTIONS
424 Craigflower Rd (388-0644; fax: 388-0636)
Hours: Mon–Fri noon–6

A bulk distributor of incense and other exotic scents; sticks and cones are $4, oils $6. (We even found a "flavour" called "black opium" here. Hmmm.)

Cheques

SHAKLEE
Elizabeth Gajan: 1–1116 Leonard St (388-5869)
Judy Holt: 2651 Rainville Rd (478-6124)
Margaret Deane: 125 Werra Rd (479-2248)
Spencer Andrews and Tara Roden: 2704 Fernwood Ave (598-7555)
Sidney: Garry & Kathy Clarke: 8531 Burgoyne Pl (656-9971)
Hours: Call ahead; machines answer off-hours

These environmentally friendly and health-related products have a good reputation, so don't be put off by the Amway-style sales technique. Call one of these independent distributors for a catalogue, order and save. Prices are lower if you become a Shaklee distributor yourself. Among the stock: Vitamin supplements, protein supplements, household cleaners, shampoos, cream rinses, toothpaste, moisturizers and other skin care products, cosmetics, makeup and water filtration systems.

Cheques

SILK ROAD
1624 Government St (383-8136)
Hours: Tue–Sat 11–5:30

These "apothecarists" create and sell aromatic plant elixirs, "botanical mists," foaming bath nectars, massage oils, mineral seabaths, the Phoenix line of skin, hair and body care products and "herbal energetics," and teas said to revitalize the spirit. A sample of one of their "legendary tea blends from the herbalist's kitchen" is free when you visit.

Cheques, Credit cards

CHILDREN'S AND INFANT NEEDS

DISCOUNT DIAPERS GALORE & MORE

Langford: 861 Station Rd (474-BABY)

Hours: Mon–Sat 9:30–5 (or later by appointment)

Disposable diapers and factory seconds at great prices—$28.99 to $35.99 per case. Cloth diapers start at $19.99 per dozen. Major lines include Babykins, Bummis, Gerber and Polliwog. If you're housebound, they'll deliver for $3.

Credit cards

DRUG NEEDS, VITAMINS, EMERGENCY FIRST AID, SUPPLEMENTS, SUNDRIES, ACUPUNCTURE & WALKING/MOBILITY AIDS

AARONSON'S PHARMACY

1089 Fort St (388-5181)

Hours: Mon–Fri 9–5:30

A full range of earthquake and disaster survival packs is available here in sizes geared to individuals or groups of up to four people. Aaronson's also stocks replacement water and food, all at competitive prices.

Credit cards

COLUMBIA FIRE & SAFETY

768 Spruce Ave (386-6773; fax: 386-3941)

Hours: Mon–Fri 8–5; Sat 9–4

Randy Miller runs this user-friendly source for all kinds of first aid items, emergency equipment, rain gear and fire and safety equipment. There are work boots, rubber boots, rubber work gloves of every kind, rescue and emergency blankets, eyewash, Dettol (in giant economy sizes), ear plugs, safety masks, signal horns and lots more. Miller will recharge your home fire extinguisher for $15.49 (2-1/2 pound size).

Credit cards, InterAc

FAIRFIELD PHARMACY
3–313 Cook St (386-6171)
Hours: Mon–Fri 9–6; Sat 10–4

This is a good place for sales in everything from cosmetics, to vitamins, to first aid to coffee. Watch newspapers for their ads.

Cheques, Credit cards

HUA REN CHINESE HERBS & ACUPUNCTURE
648 Fisgard St (380-2988)
Hours: Mon–Sat 9:30–5:30

Acupuncture sessions are $45; call for an appointment. Herb consultation prices vary but are quite inexpensive.

Cash only

INDEPENDENCE MEDICAL SUPPLY
607 Vancouver St (361-4100)
Hours: Mon–Fri 9–5

Need a new or used scooter? Walking aids? Sports medicine devices? For anyone who has ever suffered a neck or back injury, here's the place to buy (or rent) a "TENS" unit. There are also items for bathroom safety and back care, and a full line of wheelchairs. Long distance inquiries may be dialed toll-free: 1-800-665-4115.

Cheques

INTERNATIONAL COLLEGE OF TRADITIONAL CHINESE MEDICINE
108–1208 Wharf St (388-4266)
Hours: Mon–Fri 11–6

This is an accredited school that is even authorized to accept ICBC claims. It offers a free consultation with advanced students (all under clinic supervision), and if you opt for a student treatment session, it's bargain-priced at just $20.

Cash only

NATURE'S FARE
Fairfield Plaza, 6–1516 Fairfield Rd (592-3136)
Hours: Mon–Fri 9–9; Sat 9–5:30; Sun 9:30–5

Nature's Fare claims to have the largest selection of organic produce and foods, vitamins and supplements and beauty aids of any natural food store on the Island, and we don't doubt them for a minute. As well, we've found prices very fair and their weekly specials (check community newspapers for these) to be excellent. The staff are also remarkably knowledgeable about their products and will not talk you into something you don't need.

Cheques

THE RUBBER RAINBOW CONDOM CO.
Market Square, 9–560 Johnson St (388-3532; fax: 380-5005)
Hours: Mon–Sat 10–5; Sun 11–5

What can we say about this place that thousands haven't wished to say before us? (Other than that this store is an idea whose time has come.) The store is dubbed "a world of condoms," and what a world it is: There's "Slippery Stuff" personal lubricant next to custom gift packs, and many inexpensive gift condoms for every potentially embarrassing party moment you can imagine. Rubber Rainbow also sells (discreetly) by mail order and will ship everywhere. Postal code is V8W 3C6.

Credit cards

SELF-HEAL HERBS
1106 Blanshard St (383-1913)
Hours: Mon–Fri 10–5:30; Sat 10–5

Herbs, vitamins, essential oils and free advice are dispensed here as part of owner Don Ollsin's personal mission. Ollsin's association with herbs traces back to 1969. In 1976, he established this shop, originally a small herbal dispensary above a book store. Now, with his wife Sandy, this thriving business is in the heart of downtown, its catalogue vast and extensive. Automatic discounts are given for bulk orders: For purchases over $25 take off 10%; over $50, take off 15%; over $75, discount 20%. and over $100, you'll save 25%. For self-heal tinctures and teas, buy three and the fourth is free. They will also sell by mail and offer a full home study course. Write to Sandy or Don Ollsin, P.O. Box 38056, 794 Fort St., Victoria, V8W 1H2.

Credit cards

THE VITAMIN SHOP

1212 Broad St (386-1212; fax: 386-1211)

Hours: Mon–Fri 9–6; Sat 9:30–5

Virtually every one of our local insider-tipsters raved about the deals at this place, which bills itself as "Victoria's Brand Name Vitamin Dispensary." Indeed, it stocks most familiar brand names, such as Quest, Sisu, Flora, Natural Factors, Trophic, NHF, nu-life and Swiss Herbal, in both vitamins and health supplements. Upstairs in its health centre, trained staff offer athletic counselling, hair analysis, iridology and live blood assessment, and a one-hour general health assessment is free, if you make an appointment in advance. All vitamins are sold at discount prices, and seniors receive an additional reduction. Find The Vitamin Shop between Yates and Eatons. They will sell by mail order. Postal code is V8W 2A5.

Cheques, Credit cards, InterAc

EYEWEAR: EYEGLASSES & CONTACT LENS

DIAMOND OPTICAL

1320 Douglas St (380-6919)

Hours: Mon–Fri 9:30–5:30; Sat 10–5

Diamond Optical offers many deals—like hearing aid batteries for $4.50 a pack (Premium Zinc Air, Ray-o-vacs, in all sizes), and regularly price selected designer frames at 25 to 50% off (with purchase of complete eyeglasses). Also priced low are daily wear and flexi-wear soft contacts.

Credit cards

TRU-VALU OPTICAL

1708 Douglas St (386-6622)

Hours: Mon–Sat 9:30–5:30

This family-owned and -operated store bills itself as "the original discount store, often copied, never equalled." Its single-vision, frame and glasses package price is usually at $79.99, and there are other deals on specialty lenses, trifocals, no-line bifocals and more.

Credit cards

HAIRDRESSING, BARBERS & PERSONAL GROOMING SERVICES

ACT II HAIR STUDIO
207 – 3749 Shelbourne St (477-4222)
Hours: Mon–Wed & Fri & Sat 9–5; Th 9–9

This place offers a "Studentsave" reduction of 10% as part of the National Student Discount Program.

Credit cards

ACADEMY OF EXCELLENCE
1119 Fort St (386-3621)
Hours: Mon–Fri 8:30–last appt at 4 (see text)

A registered trade school since 1962, here's the place to save money by having one of their supervised students cut and style your hair. A wash and blow-dry is a mere $6.50, a cut $10. Your first perm is $25 and the second, which includes a conditioning treatment, is $29. Permanent and other "tech" work is scheduled daily from 9 to 1.

Cheques

ADVANCE SCHOOL OF HAIRDRESSING
105 – 1633 Hillside Ave (592-3245)
Hours: Mon–Fri 9–5 (Seniors, see text)

Full salon services are provided at this training facility for both men and women clients. A shampoo and cut costs $8 (add $3.50 for a blow-dry); a shampoo, set and cut is $12; and perms range in cost from $21 to $35 depending on the length of hair. Colour work costs $19 for semi-permanent toners, and ranges from $22 to $29 for permanent colour, again depending on hair length. Seniors get $1 off the shampoo, set and cut price if they book appointments for Tuesday or Wednesday.

Cheques

CUTTING BENCH CRIMPERS
1841 Fort St (595-2423)
4011 Quadra St (744-3044)

Mariner Village Mall (656-0752)
2816 Jacklin Rd (474-3241)
103 – 300 Gorge Rd W (361-4948)
Hours: Mon, Tue & Sat 9–6; Wed–Fri 9–8

Tuesdays are "tech nights" at the Gorge Road shop, where apprentices usually practise techniques and work on friends and family for free. There's no charge for a cut (just make sure you leave a nice tip), and colouring costs just $6, which merely covers the replacement cost of the chemicals. One warning, though: If you can get an appointment for a tech night, you have to settle for whatever they're practising—no special requests. Everyday prices at the other salons are reasonable: A ladies' cut is $16.82, a man's is $14.95, kids aged 9 to 12 have their hair cut for $13.08, and under 8's squirm through the experience for only $8.41. These prices include shampoo, conditioner and finish (set or blow-dry), but not taxes.

Credit cards, Cash only on tech nights

FOCUS 5000 HAIR DESIGNERS
1205 Blanshard St (385-6621)
Sidney: 2527 Beacon Ave (656-8122)
Hours: Mon–Wed 9–6; Th & Fri 9–7:30; Sat 9–5:15

Our friend Marilyn Wargo tipped us to this place, where there's a large selection of hair care products available in refillable containers at discounted prices. Regular customers are given an annual discount coupon so they can save money on their first visit of the new year—kind of a Christmas "thank you" to their steady clients.

Cheques, Credit cards

HAIR HUT
1036 Hillside Ave (383-2041)
Hours: Mon–Sat 10:30–4:30

Here's a salon offering everyday bargains, plain and simple: Haircuts are only $9.

Cash only

INTERNATIONAL HAIRDRESSING SCHOOL
705 Johnson St (386-7233, 386-6841)
Hours: Mon–Fri 8:30–4:30

Most of the time, you can just drop in here for an inexpensive haircut, but toward the end of the week it's wise to book ahead. Haircuts cost $6.50, a shampoo and cut is $10, shampoo and set is $6.50 ($7.50 for long hair), and perms—including conditioning—start at $28. Colour work is $20 (again, more for long hair).

Cheques, Credit cards

MARTIER SCHOOL OF HAIR & BEAUTY
2713 Quadra St (383-9343)
Hours: Mon–Fri 9–5; Sat 9–1

This one offers advanced makeup and haircutting courses, and it even does sculptured nails and non-surgical face lifts. The shampoo and set costs $6, as does a haircut. Colour work starts at $25. Perms are a deal: A long-hair spiral perm runs about $45—at least 50% less than what you'd expect to pay elsewhere. Gift certificates are available.

Cheques, Credit cards

PIVOT POINT INTERNATIONAL HAIRDRESSING SCHOOL
705 Johnson St (386-7233, 386-6841)
Hours: Mon–Fri 8:30–4:30

Students are closely supervised here as they perform salon services ranging from haircuts for $6.50 through perms for $35 and up (including cut and blow-dry). A simple wash and blow-dry costs $7.50; colour work (including finishing) runs about $20. The school was established in 1968.

Cheques, Credit cards

VILLAGE FLAIR HAIR STYLISTS
2232 Oak Bay Ave (598-5532)
Hours: Mon–Sat 9–5

Our pal Jan Townsend—and mother of two young children—finds this place "cheap and good" and the staff particularly adept at cutting kids' hair.

Cheques

NOTES:

6. HOME BUILDING, INTERIORS & REMODELLING

BUILDING MATERIALS, HARDWARE, TOOLS, RECYCLING, REFINISHING

When shopping in this category, we recommend that you always call ahead. The smaller places often change locations, while, strangely, some of the larger ones are notoriously hard to find. It's always wise to call around for prices anyway, especially if you're after something obscure or unusual. Please note that prices, where quoted, were accurate when we went to press, but are certainly subject to change.

We find the loss-leaders at major lumber and building supply stores excellent. Watch flyers for top values in tools and building supply savings. Many of these places will match each other's advertised specials, too, so it always helps to bring along the community flyers.

ARBUTUS STAINED GLASS
Vic West: 434 William St (384-0406)
Hours: by appointment

Local artisan Debra Snider has been creating original stained glass for years. Most of her work is designed to be consistent with its surroundings, so her Art Nouveau take-off for that replacement sidelight next to your front door can be custom-made to meld with the historical look of your home. Naturally enough, in this factory location in Vic West, Snider sells at direct-to-consumer prices.

Cheques

ARTISAN MOULDING WAREHOUSE
477 Boleskine Rd (475-2077)
Hours: Mon–Fri 8–5; Sat 9–4:30

Over 300 moulding "profiles" (designs) in oak or fir are available here at factory-direct prices. Traditional and authentic heritage styles are available.

Cheques, Credit cards

BARCLAY'S EXCHANGE
2111 Douglas St (381-4466; fax: 381-4465)
Hours: Mon–Fri 9–5:30; Sat 9–5

About the only place we could locate that buys, sells and trades used tools, Barclay's also carries stereos, TVs, compressors, chainsaws, cameras and jewellery.

Credit cards, InterAc

THE BATHTUB DOCTOR
2814 "C" Leigh Rd (478-3900)
Hours: Daily, 24 hours (machine in off-hours)

This is the original reglazing specialist for tubs, sinks and porcelain fixtures. The standard price for redoing the inside of a clawfoot tub is $350, for the outside $50. The good doctor repairs chips, too.

Cheques

BATHTUB KING
871 Marigold Rd (479-1101)
Hours: Call for free estimate 24 hours (machine)

Save the cost of new fixtures by resurfacing tubs, sinks, ceramic tile, tub surrounds and the like. The work only takes a few hours, and there are many colour choices.

Cheques

BEAVER LUMBER
1580 Hillside Ave (595-1225)
Hours: Mon–Fri 8:30–9; Sat 8:30–5:30; Sun 10–5

We still find the flyer specials here among the best values in town, and we like the fact that they stand behind their products. We had a faulty tape measure—and no receipt—and they exchanged it for a good one, no questions asked and no hassle. That's service.

Credit cards

C.W.W.P. LTD
925 Dunford Ave (474-4733)
Hours: Mon–Fri 8–5:30; Sat 9–4

What acts like wood (takes a nail, screw, saws, etc.), yet costs less, never needs painting, won't rot and is insect proof? Why, it's 100% plastic lumber, made from recycled materials and totally environmentally friendly. Not only does it not decompose in the rain and against bare earth, but it won't leach harmful chemicals into the soil if you use it for garden posts or to edge raised beds, etc. It's perfect for wharfs, decking, landscaping, fencing, picnic tables and benches. Available sizes are currently limited, but more will be produced as demand grows. Colours are compatible with the uses we've mentioned.

Cheques, Credit cards

CAPITAL IRON
1900 Store St (385-9703)
Langford: 770 Goldstream (474-5601)
Sidney: 2353 Bevan Ave (655-7115)
Hours: Mon–Sat 9–5:30; Sun 11–5 (all locations)

Dating back to its days in 1934 as a scrap yard, everyone's favourite "general store" in Victoria is the Capital Iron headquarters in a charming old heritage building on the waterfront. Here you'll find earthquake emergency supplies, hunting and fishing gear, nautical goods, fabric, hardware, collectibles, surplus, housewares, electrical supplies, gardening stuff, outerwear, jeans, upholstery and sewing machines (and the repairs to go with them).

Credit cards

COLONIAL COUNTERTOPS
646 Alpha St (383-1926, 383-3953; fax: 383-4425)
Hours: Mon–Fri 8–5; Sat 10–3

Another factory-direct outlet, this one (established in 1970) sells the countertops to go with your discount cabinets. There's no wait for delivery, either, as they have a large inventory on hand. Costs start as low as $8 per lineal foot.

Credit cards

COOK STREET DO-IT CENTER
1720 Cook St (384-8181)
Hours: Mon–Fri 8–5:30; Sat 9–5:30; Sun 10–5

This is a favourite of ours, perhaps because we never got over seeing those beautiful Rubbermaid Adirondack chairs on sale when they first came to market—which is an interesting aspect of the Do-It Centre's marketing philosophy: They'll often reduce new products just when they appear on to the scene, instead of having an end-of-season sale like so many other places. Their sale flyers frequently appear as supplements to the newspaper, and their specials are consistently excellent—like the $5.99 clean-up kit: scrub brush, Simple Green soap packet, 3 foam sponges, wiping cloth, two polishing cloths and a no-scratch scrub pad, or the brass-finish, three-lamp set for $89.99. Everyday prices on paint, electricals, ladders and builders' tools are competitive, too.

Credit cards

CRYSTAL BATHTUB RE-GLAZE
Address unavailable (388-0572)
Hours: Call machine 24 hours

Here's a service that not only saves you the cost of replacing a worn bathtub or sink, but also promises you a 20–30% saving (compared to their competitors) on the cost of the work itself.

Cheques

THE FINISHING TOUCH
780 Topaz St (384-3003; fax: 384-3635)
Hours: Mon–Fri 8–5; Sat 9–5

We wonder whether this is as good a deal for the home handyperson as it once was, yet we find their specials compelling, and it's certainly the place to find precisely the kind of moulding you require for a small job. There's usually a clear-out bin of small cuts that are ideal for modest craft projects, and the quality of their doors, wood flooring and shelving is beyond compare. For long distance estimates, call their toll-free line at 1-800-665-1560.

Credit cards

G.W.G. RENTALS
1939 Keating X Rd (652-3908)
Hours: Mon–Fri 7:30–5; Sat 8–5

You'll find Keating X Road on the road to Butchart Gardens, on the way to Patricia Bay. G.W.G. rents large tools, U-hauls—in fact, says the owner, "everything for the contractor or homeowner." They also offer reasonable repairs and parts.

Credit cards

INTERNATIONAL KNIVES & DARTS (woodcarving tools)—See Sporting Goods

ISLAND MARBLE
6829 Veyaness Road (652-2680)
Hours: Mon–Fri 8–4:30; Sat 9–4

Island Marble offers one thing we find irresistible: A one-day factory clearance sale, usually after their buyers have returned from one of the Island's (or Lower Mainland's) big home shows. These items include bathtubs, enclosures, jacuzzis, vanity tops, splash guards, shower stalls and plumbing fixtures, factory seconds, customer returns and many one-of-a-kinds, all at 50–90% off. Call ahead to find out when the next sale is due, and keep in mind that even their everyday prices are factory-direct.

Cheques

LUMBERWORLD
3955 Quadra St (479-7151)
Hours: Mon–Sat 7:30–5:30

Here's a good source of tools, lighting and electrical supplies, plus regular specials on lumber and building supplies. Watch the newspaper for ads that include loss-leader coupons, like the snap-blade knife we spotted recently for 47 cents (limit two, with coupon).

Credit cards

O.B.O. SALVAGE
526 Discovery St (389-6200)
Hours: Mon–Fri 9–5:30; Sat & Sun 9–8

This newly relocated recycling place is a great outlet for high-quality used building supplies, doors, light fixtures and windows.

Cheques

OLD CANADIAN U-LOAD CONTAINERS
Address unavailable (386-8376)
Hours: 24 hours, see text

Elizabeth and Rocky run this small, family business from their home. Their U-load containers are affordable for even small-scale renovation jobs. With a little notice, they'll deliver a dumpster to your worksite (rental is $100 and duration of rental is quite flexible—all for that same, flat fee), then remove it and take the rubbish to the dump. Each load of debris carted away costs an extra $75 (dumping fee), and they ask that you separate gyprock from the other trash. If there's very little gyprock to discard, set it on top of the load (and try to keep it from getting wet), so it's easier to remove.

Cheques

PAY 'N' PACK CABINETS (countertops)—See Cabinets & Closet Organizers

PRESTIGE JOINERY
434 William St (384-0406)
Hours: Mon–Fri 8–5; Sat by appt

This is our friend James Townsend's workshop, where he and his partners fashion authentic, heritage-style doors and windows from fine woods. Some doors have etched glass, relief carving or other details, and some include stained glass made to match a home's existing motif by on-premises artisan Debra Snider. Though prices at Prestige may seem dear, they're a bargain considering the quality of workmanship and attention to detail. This is factory-direct, after all.

Cheques

SAVE-A-TUB
2120 Oak Bay Ave (380-6766)
Hours: 24-hour machine

These folks promise savings of 20–50% and more on the cost of replacement tubs, sinks, tiles, fridges and stoves—all through the magic of reglazing. They can even resurface countertops with the same no-mess process. As well, if you really do want to replace your old tub, they make a sideline out of buying, restoring and selling Victorian claw-foot tubs.

Cheques

STUCCO DOCTOR
Address unavailable (744-3545)
Hours: 24-hour machine

We can't help but wonder if his mom gets to refer to him as "my son, the doctor," but his work must be excellent, because he offers his "patients" a lifetime guarantee on the work. Restucco work is supposed to make the exterior surface of your home denser and more water resistant than conventional stucco or cement surfaces that are already painted, so you'll save in the long run by eliminating costly repairs and repainting. The finished work is available in more than 200 colours. The process costs about the same as a professional paint job.

Cheques

SUPER DAVE'S ENTERPRISES (counters)—See Kitchen Equipment

SURPLUS CITY
517 Herald St (388-7172)
Hours: Mon–Sat 9–6; Sun 10–5

Bookcases, cabinets, replacement windows and doors, furniture and architectural salvage all appear from time to time in manufacturers' clearouts, bankruptcies and liquidations at Surplus City.

Credit cards

THUNDERBIRD
2929 Douglas St (386-2921; fax: 386-2450)
Hours: Mon–Wed 8:30–5:30; Th & Fri 8:30–9; Sat 9–5:30; Sun 10–5

Colwood: 1736 Island Hwy (478-1942; fax: 478-9566)
Hours: Mon–Th 8:30–5:30; Fri 8:30–9; Sat 9–5:30; Sun 10–5

Thunderbird is another big name where we've occasionally been disappointed by high prices, yet found great flyer bargains when we checked around for prices. The new location, which opened near the beginning of 1994, certainly offered some superior deals as opening specials, plus all kinds of freebies to entice home repair buffs. We can only hope they keep it up. Stock includes cabinets, doors, electrical, hardware, plumbing supplies and more.

Credit cards

TOOLS 'N SPACE
338 Catherine St (383-9600; fax: 383-0422)
Hours: Tue–Sat 10–5

A great idea for the apartment-dweller or novice woodworker, this place offers both classes in do-it-yourself furniture making and the space in which to complete your projects. They carry a huge range of woodworking tools, lathes, power tools and specialty woodworking books. There's free parking, and you can visit next door at Spinnaker's Pub while the glue dries on that Cape Cod chair kit ($109). Woodworking videos rent for $7.95 for one video, $5.95 for additionals. There's a good assortment of clock and toy parts, plus many hardwood and exotic veneers. Beginner classes start at regular intervals.

Credit cards

VINTAGE WOODWORKS
408 Alpha Terrace (386-5354)
Hours: Mon–Fri 9–5 (showroom); 7–3:30 (shop)

This firm offers an affordable way to double-glaze windows, a method that allows you to open, close and lock from the inside (added security) and enables you to extend the life of existing windows with unique wooden storm windows.

Cheques

WE HAUL CHEAP
Address unavailable (384-1145)
Hours: Call 24 hr (machine answers during off-hours)

Round-the-clock service makes it possible to have refuse hauled away from your work site with a minimum of fuss—and the materials are recycled, so you're doing your part for the environment.

Cheques

WEATHER WISE INDUSTRIES
2126 Keating X Rd (652-4474)
Hours: Mon–Fri 7:30–5:30; Sat 8–5

Here's the only place we know of to buy pre-fabricated cedar fence panels in kits from $40 (for 4x8 panels; assembled from $46). They also do installations. We figure these prices to be about 40% off our neighbourhood lumberyard, since Weather Wise advertises "Direct from our mills to you."

Cheques, Credit cards

WESTBURNE
872 Cloverdale Ave
Plumbing & Heating: 475-1111

Bath & Lighting: 475-1120
Electrical: 475-1900
Hours: Mon–Fri 7–4:30

Westburn is a reliable source for building materials every day, but periodically, they come up with a dilly of a sale: A one-day blowout of bathroom and lighting items, up to 80% off regular prices. Call ahead to find out when the next sale is planned, or watch local papers for ads.

Cheques, Credit cards, InterAc

WINDSOR PLYWOOD
2120 Keating X Rd (652-5632)
Hours: Mon–Fri 8–5; Sat 8:30–5

Locally owned, Windsor sells a full range of lumber and building supplies, plus name brand saw blades, router bits and all kinds of tools. Periodically, they run newspaper ads offering 20% off your purchases—if you bring in the ad.

Cheques, Credit cards

WINNCRAFT WOOD PRODUCTS (shelving, cabinets)—See Furniture

CABINETS & CLOSET ORGANIZERS

CABINET DEPOT
611 Dunedin St (388-9123)
Hours: Tue–Fri 10–6; Sat 10–5

Cabinets for every room at prices starting from $199 for a 5-cabinet starter kitchen; even the 11-cabinet job for a small kitchen costs only $329. They also make and sell a variety of closet organizers you can install yourself. This is a true warehouse operation, relatively new to Victoria. Sales staff are friendly and eager for your business.

Credit cards

CASH & CARRY CABINET WAREHOUSE
800 Cloverdale Ave (475-1159)
Hours: Mon–Fri 9–5; Sat 10–3

They claim to sell all manner of cabinets and vanities here for about 50% off retail elsewhere. We suggest you shop around for the best deal, but be sure to put this place on your list when you compare prices. Very low overhead, due partly to nearly invisible staff; we had trouble getting anyone's attention. Once you do buy, however, they promise a 5-year warranty and everything's fully assembled.

Cheques, Credit cards

THE FINISHING TOUCH—**See Building Materials**

HOMETOWN CABINET FACTORY
2655 Rock Bay Ave (384-0099)
Hours: Mon–Sat 9–5

They stock everything from closet towers (80x16x16, from $79) to custom modular systems ("order as many drawers as you like") to full kitchen ensembles from $1874; this locally made kitchen grouping, for instance, includes lazy susan, double sink cabinet, super-deep pots and pans drawer, pantry/broom closet/utility cabinet, adjustable shelves, and is available in white, almond or grey melamine finish, fully assembled.

Cheques, Credit cards

MATTHEWS AGENCIES SHELVING & STORE FIXTURES
776-778 Spruce Ave (388-4123; fax: 383-5168)
Hours: Mon–Fri 8:30–4:30

We've often found that store fixture suppliers carry better quality shelving, chrome grids, bins and clothing racks—for lower prices—than do the actual closet organizer stores. Find this outlet right across from Canadian Tire (easy parking out front), but note they are not open on weekends.

Cheques, Credit cards

PAY-LESS CABINETS
416 Garbally Rd (380-0727)
Hours: Mon–Fri 8–5; Sat 9–4

Formerly called Cash & Carry Discount Cabinets, this outfit changed its name, they told us, "because another company was cashing in on our advertising." The situation was pretty confusing, but rest assured—it still offers the same great deals. Pay-Less operates as a division of Harbour City Kitchen and sells its cabinets at rock-bottom, factory-direct prices. Their fully-assembled, white melamine laundry cabinets or vanity cabinets start at $50 each, and they have a large selection of factory seconds in mix-and-match combos (plus PVC-faced units), all at low prices. Their closet organizers start at $75 (for a 15-inch width by 16-inch deep, full-height unit) and optional drawers (from $35) or extra shelves and hanger rods are also available cheaply.

Cheques, Credit cards

PAY 'N' PACK CABINETS
464 Burnside Rd E (382-9494; fax: 382-9491)
Hours: Mon–Th 8–5:30; Fri 8–5; Sat 9–4

Now located in the Old Winery where Fuzzy Wuzzy Carpets used to be, this place boasts hundreds of European kitchen and bathroom cabinets in stock—fully assembled and ready for installation—at factory direct prices (50% off retail). They also stock countertops, also at cash-and-carry prices.

Cheques, Credit cards

SUPER DAVE'S ENTERPRISES (shelving)—See Kitchen Equipment

FLOOR COVERINGS

This is another area where it really pays to shop around for price and quality—by phone and flyers—before heading out. It also helps to prepare yourself for high-pressure sales tactics in most of the stores in this category; you'll quickly sense which stores have sales staff on commission and which don't.

BOB ALEXANDER'S S & A CARPET COVE
643 David Street (382-8231)
Hours: Mon–Th 9–5; Fri 9–6; Sat & Sun 9–4

Here we've discovered good-quality roll-ends, linos, carpets and periodic blow-out sales that make even their end-of-lines prices (which are already low) look high. Certainly one to put on your price-comparison list, and if you find what you need here (a laundry-room-sized roll-end, for instance), you're in business.

Cheques, Credit cards

FUZZY-WUZZY CARPETS
3460A Quadra St (380-9000, 380-9800; fax 380-9533)
Hours: Mon–Th & Sat 9–5:30; Fri 9–9

Moved last year to new premises, this Victoria landmark doesn't just sell carpets these days, but offers a full range of builders' supplies, paint, wallcoverings and more, all at low prices. They claim to be "Vancouver Island's largest discount carpet centre," with over 2,000 roll ends and remnants, name brand carpets and linos and hundreds of rolls in stock in over 9,000 square feet of showroom and warehouse space. Easy wheelchair access, by the way.

Cheques, Credit cards

JORDANS CARPET CLEARANCE CENTRE
3090-D Nanaimo St (385-5551)
Hours: Mon–Fri 8–5; Sat 9–5; Sun noon–5

Calling itself "Victoria's Discount Flooring Centre," Jordans is exactly that: Contractors' overs, full rolls and remnants in a constantly changing stock are all priced to clear. They carry all major lines, plus roll-ends and lino. Periodically, they run clearance sales to make room for more stock.

Credit cards

RUG CUTTERS
585 Bay St (480-1612)
Hours: Mon–Fri 9–5; Sat 10–4:30

Yet another "carpet clearance warehouse", this one always has new carpet roll ends in abundance and periodically runs a clear-out sale with even deeper price cuts. Formerly known as E M Carpet Manufacturers Clearance Warehouse. They also rent aisle-runners for weddings.

Cheques

SLEGG LUMBER (carpets)—See Furniture

TILE CENTRE
2324 Government St (383-8121)
Hours: Mon–Fri 8:30–5:30; Sat 9–5

The large inventory here includes ceramic floor tiles, white marble, mosaics, bevelled designer wall tiles, terra cotta tiles, borders and ceramic edging, all at rock-bottom prices. They are also inclined to run a "total floor clearance" sale periodically with further reductions to 30–60% off.

Credit cards

TILE TOWN
3098 Nanaimo St (385-2141)
Hours: Mon–Fri 8:30–5:30; Sat 9–5; Sun 10–4

The hook here is "factory-direct imports" and, presumably, factory-direct prices. Colours and styles are limited on the clear-out stock, but they do maintain a fairly large inventory and their sale prices are excellent. Coupons appear in the newspaper offering limited-time extra-specials, like free Thinset bonding mortar with every purchase of 100 square feet (or more) of in-stock, regular-priced floor tile. Bring such coupons along to take advantage of the deal.

Credit cards

UNITED CARPET
758 Cloverdale (475-3811)
Sidney: 9752 4th St (655-4858)
Hours: Mon–Fri 8:30–5:30; Sat 8:30–5

Their everyday prices are really competitive, but their annual blowout sales (often early in February) are legendary, with slogans like "With prices this low, you'd think we're out of our minds." Never mind the hype—they really do offer good deals, and it seems there's always something on sale, from carpeting to mini-blinds, to hardwood flooring, ceramic tile, lino, area rugs and more. They offer a written, lifetime warranty on any installation they do themselves.

Credit cards

PAINT & WALLPAPER

Paint and wallpaper stores operate in a very competitive business, so sales really mean something. To gain the edge over their competition, many stores have decorating experts on hand (or they bring them to the Island from time to time), and some have entire mock-window set-ups in the store and free demos to show renovators how, for instance, to apply wallpaper around mouldings. Some have instructional videos free-for-the-borrowing, if you'll buy their products. Watch for closeout bins and annual sales in wallpaper stores. We suggest you browse for wallpaper before the sales, when all is quiet and you can scan books without interruption or distraction. Then, when sale time arrives, place your order and save from 20–30%. Most wallpaper stores will tell you when their sales occur (usually semi-annually), so you can plan ahead.

Paint stores have their own version of the closeout bin, often referred to as the "boneyard". Boneyard cans are usually half off because the wrong shade was produced (called a "mismatch"). Overstocks and old colours will also be cleared out on a casual basis, as compared to advertised sale periods. If you don't readily spot the boneyard, ask if there are any discontinued or mismatched cans on hand. It's unusual not to find at least a few in any store where paint is mixed and sold. For larger projects, we suggest you check out small, local manufacturers and distributors. Sometimes you can only buy at these places through a contractor, and sometimes it's okay if you're acting as your own contractor, which is a legitimate practice nowadays. You will have to be the final judge of the quality you require. Paints, like floor-coverings, vary considerably in quality and price, and well-advertised labels are not necessarily superior to locally produced products. Most paint outlets will allow you a "contract discount" if you purchase in quantity (minimum 5 gallons) and only if you ask for a discount. Standard contract discount is 20%, but you can do better if you purchase still larger quantities.

CLOVERDALE PAINT
3088 Blanshard St (382-6148)
Hours: Mon–Th 7–5:30; Fri 7–9; Sat 8:30–5; Sun 10–4

Colwood: 1913 Sooke Rd (478-5525)
Hours: Mon–Fri 7:30–5:30; Sat 8:30–5; Sun 10–4

Sidney: 9768 5th St (656-3975)
Hours: Mon–Fri 7:30–5:30; Sat 8–5:30; Sun 10–4

Flyers announce sale prices on virtually all Cloverdale paints and wallpapers at some point or other during the year, reducing their already low prices to sometimes quite extraordinary levels. Wallpaper and borders, for instance, are generally 30–50% off suggested retail, everyday, and when sale time rolls around, they take off a further 30%. And we've seen a good quality interior latex sale priced for as little as $9.88 for a 3.78 litre pail (what used to pass for a gallon). They also promise a "no hassle" guarantee.

Credit cards

EMPRESS PAINTING
15 – 1594 Fairfield Rd (383-5224)
Hours: call the cellular phone 7:30–7:30

Owner Phil Cameron does mainly commercial work, but when our friends Cary and Marilyn were shopping around for the best deal to have their house painted, they chose Empress because they felt they'd get a square deal. Phil gave them three levels of quote, depending on how finicky a job they wanted (they chose the middle quote). All the work includes power-washing and surface prep work, plus a different length of solid guarantee for each level of quote. They had their entire (large) home painted inside and out, and a year later they have no complaints.

Payment terms may be arranged

FUZZY-WUZZY CARPETS (paint)—See Floor Coverings

INDUSTRIAL PLASTICS & PAINT
3944 Quadra St (727-3545, 1-800-667-1757; fax: 727-7066)
Hours: Mon–Sat 8–5:30

Probably Victoria's favourite local source for paint and paint bargains, Industrial focuses on top-grade SICO paints. They also stock everything for the amateur or professional house painter: Drop cloths, rollers, ladders, clean-up equipment and more. And their sales are legendary—watch newspapers for ads. Out-of-towners needing info or quotes can call 1-800-667-1757 toll-free.

Cheques, Credit cards

PACIFIC PAINT & WALLPAPER
1031 Hillside Ave (381-5254)
Hours: Mon–Fri 7:30–6; Sat 9–5

Another solid choice for paint-purchase savings, this one features Benjamin Moore paints and the company's computerized colour-matching system for flawless choice of hue. Their annual anniversary sale usually runs in May.

Cheques, Credit cards

VINTAGE PAINTING
309 Brunswick Place (360-8860)
Hours: 24-hour machine

This firm specializes in renovating and painting heritage homes. Owners Mike and Bob, with 25 years' experience, give free estimates.

Cheques

WALLPAPER PLUS
477 Boleskine Rd (475-2007)
Hours: Mon–Fri 7:30–5:30; Sat 8–5

Recently relocated near Town & Country Centre, Wallpaper Plus is now combined with Walls Alive to create a super discount store. Periodic sales are offered on paint, wallpapers, matching papers and fabrics from Sanderson, and most of the stock of co-ordinated drapery and upholstery fabrics. They carry a range of name brands and offer free decorating consultation.

Credit cards

WALLS ALIVE—See Wallpaper Plus, above

WINDOW COVERINGS & STAINED GLASS

ARBUTUS STAINED GLASS—See Building Materials

CONTOUR WINDOW FASHIONS
211 – 3214 Douglas St (475-3221)
Hours: Mon–Sat 9:30–5:30

As Canada's largest blind and drapery specialist, Contour Window Fashion is able to offer consumers a good deal by dint of its sales volume. Contour periodically offers 30–50% discounts on Levelor blinds (one of several top-notch brands). Another offering is the "full house deal," whereby you can save more if you order custom blinds for eight windows or more. (Periodically, they hold a 50% off retail sale; call ahead for dates.) Contour also stocks verticals, pleated shades, micro-blinds, woven wood and roller shades, valences and bedding. You'll find interesting decorating ideas in their showroom, plus free in-home service and consultation. Cindy Wass-Thomas is the local rep. Be sure to ask her for free guidance in measuring your windows, so you don't make a mistake in sizing. Drapery brand names include Hunter Douglas, Window Wear, Pride of Paris, Robert Allen, Aftex and Tritex.

Cheques, Credit cards

GLASS-SMITH & CO
475 – 3311 Tennyson Ave (475-3388; fax: 475-3377)
Hours: Mon–Fri 8:30–5; Sat 9–4

Factory-direct prices are the drawing card here, where available stock ranges from windshields to artglass to custom-designed stained glass.

Cheques, Credit cards

STUDIO GLASS
842 Cormorant St (360-1701)
Hours: "By chance or by appointment"

Valla Eriksson's cast glass and kiln-form glass work results in gorgeous earrings, runes and other decorative accents, but she also creates window pendants and will make stained glass to order. She holds periodic open-house days, usually on a Sunday from noon-4, so if you're interested, call ahead for the next date or make an appointment for a consultation. We loved the Icelandic love charm she showed last time, formed in ruby glass and selling for only $7.

Credit cards

TRUEMAN DRAPERY INTERIORS
782 Spruce Ave (386-3021)
Hours: Mon–Fri 9–5; Sat 10–3

Trueman Drapery promises "award winning window fashions at factory direct prices"—up to 70% off selected designer fabrics and up to 60% off Tachikawa micro blinds (full colour range). In-home designer consultation is free. Trueman is right across from Canadian Tire, so there's ample free parking. Seniors receive a modest discount.

Cheques, Credit cards

NOTES:

7. HOME & GARDEN

FURNITURE, OLD & NEW; & FURNITURE REPAIRS/REFINISHING

BJ'S GENERAL STORE
514 Fisgard St (383-5535)
Hours: Mon–Sat 11–5 (winter): Mon–Sat 11–6; Sun 11–5 (summer)

Really, this should be called B & J's because the owners are Betty French and Judi Walters. Whatever the name (and anyway, doesn't the sign look like it says "General BJ's"?), there are lots of antique and antique-look decor accents, furniture, funk, enamel ware, kitchen linens, utensils, pottery, novelty cookie jars, teapots, tureens, unusual giftwrap, cards, spices, and some really attractive and practical unfinished stacking pine boxes. Prices are very reasonable. Adjoins Songhee's, next door.

Cheques, Credit cards

THE BRICK
2635 Quadra St (380-1133)
Hours Mon–Fri 9–9; Sat 9–6; Sun 11–5

Despite the chain's flashy flyers and unfortunately high-pressure sales people, who can sure take the fun out of shopping, there are often very good deals on furniture, appliances, TVs and stereos. Another lure is the occasional no-interest, no-down-payment, deferred payment pitch (on approval of credit, of course).

Cheques, credit cards

B & E APPLIANCE WAREHOUSE
10 – 1610 Island Hwy (474-2844)
Hours: Mon–Fri 9–5:30; Sat 9–4

Here's a popular source for new and used parts and appliances. Prices are low; choices are many and varied—always a large stock.

Credit cards

BUDGET HOME OF RENT-TO-OWN
833 Yates St (383-3655)
Hours: Mon–Fri 9–9, Sat 9–6; Sun noon–5

Furniture (of the rather low-end sort) and appliances are rented out here, and occasionally cleared out on sale. TV and VCR combos start as low as $49.95. Appliances are generally brand names —Fisher, Samsung, Zenith, Sanyo and Mitsubishi. Free, same-day delivery (O.A.C.).

Credit cards

CLICK'S FURNITURE WAREHOUSE
805 Cloverdale Ave (475-3000; fax: 475-3001)
Hours: Mon–Wed & Sat 9–5:30; Th & Fri 9–9; Sun noon–5

Top quality, name-brand furniture is sold at what the owners claim are "guaranteed lowest prices." In this warehouse operation at the corner of Blanshard St and Cloverdale Ave, there's a large inventory of beds, living room and dining room suites, occasional tables, sofas and chairs, all at prices up to 70% off retail.

Credit cards

DAVID ROBINSON ANTIQUES
1007 Langley St (384-6425)
Hours: Mon–Sat 10–4

Robinson buys, sells and consigns fine antiques at reasonable prices. His stock encompasses furniture, fine oriental rugs, clocks, silver, porcelain and paintings—plus, promises Robinson, "top prices paid."

Cheques, Credit cards

DODD'S FURNITURE
715 Finlayson TK (388-6663; fax: 388-7414)
Hours: Mon–Fri 9–9; Sat 9–6; Sun noon–5

The big drawing cards at Dodd's are mattresses: Singles with a 10-year warranty start as low as $98 (each piece) and the top-of-the-line B.C.-made Grange pillowtop single size costs only $198 (per piece). Find Dodd's in the strip mall opposite Mayfair Mall—free parking, of course. Periodic specials and door-crashers make scanning newspaper ads worthwhile.

Credit cards

FANNY DAVIS ANTIQUES
1028 Fort St (360-1889)
Hours: Mon–Sat 10–5

Fanny Davis sells reproduction pine period furniture, collectibles, jewellery, china, and she will purchase entire estates for cash.

Cheques, Credit cards

FOCUS ON PATIO
2624 Quadra St (383-8222)
Hours: Mon–Sat 9:30–5:30

Locally manufactured Sunpacific patio furniture and an extensive collection of exotic rattan and wicker, aluminum, wood and resin furniture at low prices. Five-piece dinette suites in Kiani rattan start at $499. They also carry replacement cushions and provide repairs—recovering patio umbrellas and restrapping chairs and lounges. They're right across from the Brick (easy parking). Free delivery.

Credit cards

FURNITURE MEDIC
1252 Gladstone Ave (388-7600)
Hours: 24-hr machine

The motto here: "Don't toss it away . . . repair it." The Rx Furniture Medic provides on-site repairs for scratches, stains, dents and moving damage, at "a fraction of the cost of refinishing or replacement."

Visa only

THE LIVING END
533 Fisgard St, rear (385-5677)
Hours: Call ahead for hours

Once a consignment store that carried clothing, The Living End was renovating for a July '94 opening when we went to press. They will be accepting consignment, but only on furniture.

Credit cards

LOMAS BARGAIN SHOP
2676 Quadra St (382-5221)
Hours: Daily: 9:30–5:30

At first glance we thought this was just a typical tacky secondhand store, but on closer inspection we discovered some very charming used furniture at low, low prices. Among the stock when we last pressed our noses to the windows—while waiting for the show to start at the Roxy across the street—were beds, bureaus, lamps, desks and a '40-style night-table we already regret not returning to buy.

Cheques, Credit cards

NATIONWIDE WAREHOUSE & STORAGE
1–460 Tennyson Pl (380-6006)
Hours: Mon, Th & Fri 10–8; Tue & Wed–Sat 10–6; Sun noon–5

Nationwide operates a huge warehouse store at Boleskine and Tennyson (entrance off Tennyson Ave.), with plush living room furniture, recliners, complete bedroom suites, and mattresses priced from just $78 (extra-firm, single). Brass-plated headboards —any size—start at $24.

Cheques, Credit cards

THE OAK SHOPPE
2504 Douglas St (385-1655; fax: 381-2549)
Hours: Mon–Sat 9:30–5:30; Sun 11–4

The Oak Shoppe showcases a gorgeous collection of fine oak furniture in spacious premises right on Douglas. Given the superior quality and craftsmanship of the furniture, it's surprisingly inexpensive, particularly during the annual anniversary scratch-and-dent sale, usually held in April-May. A layaway plan and financing are available. Their market position is that they are "Vancouver Island's largest retailer of oak furniture and will not be undersold. We will match or beat any competitor's advertised price." And they mean it.

Credit cards, Financing

RATTAN UNLIMITED
2333 Government St (384-3243)
Hours: Mon–Sat 9:30–6

Another of those places that always seems to have a sale of one kind or another going, this is an excellent place to buy those $9 bamboo blinds you've been seeking. A five-drawer wicker dresser was sale-priced recently at $279, and a charming white wicker chaise (cushions extra) was $169. There are also generous financing terms (O.A.C.).

Credit cards, Financing

SALLY'S ANTIQUES, COLLECTABLES & FINE OLDE FURNITURE
Colwood: 328 Goldstream Ave (478-4524)
Hours: Mon–Th 10–5:30; Fri 10–8; Sat 11–5:30; Sun 11–5

This cosy 1,800-square-foot house is crammed with fine furniture, collectibles and old pictures. At their anniversary sale in April, they offered a Victorian walnut wardrobe, with bevelled mirror door and carved panels for $349, and a Victorian walnut dressing chest with triple mirror for $249 (each less than half-price).

Cheques, Credit cards

SIX MILE FURNITURE
1612 Island Highway (474-2026)
Hours: Mon–Th & Sat 10–6; Fri 10–9; Sun noon–5

Deals we've spotted here include an attractive curio cabinet for $269 and a contemporary-styled entertainment centre for only $89.

Cheques, Credit Cards, InterAc

SLEGG LUMBER
Sidney: 2030 Malaview Ave (656-1125; fax: 655-4996)
Hours: Mon–Sat 7:30–5:30

Whittier-brand wood furniture kits are featured here, ready-to-assemble, stain and varnish. There's a full selection of tables, chairs and bookshelves, like the country table (from $143.96, sale-priced) or Pleasant Hill table ($215.96 on sale). Chairs range from the Riverside (priced from $37.56 to $46.95) to the Country bowback ($63.96 to $79.95). Slegg also carries carpets and hardwood for all your flooring needs, with periodic sale prices bringing carpets down to as little as $6.88 a square yard.

Credit cards

SONGHEES IMPORTS
516 Fisgard St (388-7769; fax; 388-6088)
Hours: Summer: Mon–Sat 10–6; Sun 11–5;
winter: Mon–Sat 11–5

Jan Parkin runs this huge store adjacent to BJ's General Store. You'll find inexpensive rattan, wicker, bamboo, brass and giftware, furniture (we saw a nice, white, four-drawer bureau for only $79), baskets, artificial flowers, lots of vertigris sundials, bookcases, birdfeeders, wooden cows, distressed watering cans, windchimes, beds, nice pine chests, and loads of low-cost (yet apparently well-made) shelving, windows and doors. A half-price table is strategically placed at the centre of the store. A great find!

Credit cards, InterAc

STANDARD FURNITURE OUTLET
800 Tolmie Ave (382-5111; fax: 381-1241)
Hours: Mon–Sat 9–5:30; Th & Fri 9–9; Sun noon–5

805 Cloverdale Ave (475-3002)

Hours: Mon–Wed & Sat 9–5:30; Th & Fri 9–9; Sun noon–5

Sidney: 202 – 9768 5th St (655-1010)

Hours: Mon–Sat 9–5:30; Sun noon–5

Of the three locations of Standard Furniture, their clearance centre is the one on Cloverdale—but there are deals to be had at each. Brand-name sofa-beds, like the one by Pallister, go for as little as $497 (sale-priced), and we've seen two-piece "silver" Sealy mattress sets priced from $379. Sales stuffers are a common feature in the local paper. Out-of-town inquiries, call toll-free 1-800-667-1314. Free delivery to Campbell River, Port Alberni and "all points south".

Cheques, Credit cards

UNITED BUY & SELL

2835 Douglas St (360-2300)

1652 Island Hwy (474-1244)

1949 Keating X Rd (652-1555)

Hours: Mon–Fri 10–9; Sat 10–6

These are furniture liquidators, so each location offers its own stock of sofas, dinettes, living room and bedroom sets, etc., and its own one-of-a-kind bargains. Mattresses are sometimes sold below wholesale and many come with extended manufacturer's warranty.

Cheques, Credit cards

VELVET TOUCH FURNITURE REFINISHING

2516 Douglas St (384-1844)

Hours: Mon–Fri 8:30–5; Sat 10–2

Their slogan, "save trees—refinish today," is catchy, and so is their policy of "no caustics, no dip tanks" and free pick-up and delivery. They even do pianos. Minimum charge for stripping is $15, $20 for repair, and touch-up work starts at $35. There's free parking at the rear.

Cheques

WINNCRAFT WOOD PRODUCTS

961 Dunford Ave (478-4702)

Hours: Mon–Fri 8–5; Sat 9–3

Manufacturer-direct discounts make this an ideal stop for wooden step stools, rocking horses, tool totes for the handyman, toy chests, storage units, mantels, ski racks, toys, bookcases and particularly corner cabinets (the latter starting as low as $39.95 for a two-foot unit). Custom inquiries are welcome. Watch for their year-end clearance (up to 30% off) and extended Boxing Day sale.

Cheques, Credit cards

WOODPECKER FURNITURE & FUTONS
1601 Douglas St (382-2771)
Hours: Mon–Sat 10–5; Sun noon–4

Jennifer Duda's family-run business (since 1974) is a fabulous shopping (and browsing) experience. There are rugs, cosy knit throws, beautiful, unfinished, solid pine furniture ("made just down the street," said Jennifer), shelves (and modular shelving), cupboards, and excellent prices for futon sofas ($299 complete for a double-size). We loved the unfinished pine boxes for $59 and had our hearts set on several of the coffee tables (also $59). There's an occasional 20% off sale of European antique pine (their other line), and sometimes a 50% off fabric sale. Everything seems high-quality and low-cost—our kind of store.

Cheques, Credit cards

HOUSEHOLD APPLIANCES & REPAIRS

Reconditioned appliances may have no more than cosmetic damage or a loose wire when returned to the factory or service centre for repair, and many of these represent huge savings over "first quality" items. Freight-damaged goods often show strictly minor, cosmetic damage that doesn't affect the working ability of the appliance. For instance, we know someone who bought a freight-damaged dishwasher (the kind that is not built-in, but rolls away when not in use) that had a minor scratch on its chopping block top—hardly a defect, in that the block was designed to stand up to being whacked with a meat cleaver! The saving on this unit alone was 50%, and the dishwasher, now long-ago passed along to friends, is still working perfectly after 20 years of daily service.

Replacement parts are also rewarding to locate and install. When our dryer's timing dial became stripped of the inside grooves that gripped the metal, we were quoted $60 for a service call from the department store from which it came. A few minutes' research on the phone yielded a parts source close to home, and the total cost of replacement came to a grand total of $1.79, including taxes!

A & A APPLIANCE SERVICES
Address unavailable (477-3622)
Hours: Daily 8 a.m.–9 p.m.

No extra charge for after hours, weekends and holidays, and they insist they work for "low, low rates". They also promise same-day service on all makes and models of fridges, stoves, freezers, dishwashers, washers and dryers (free estimates). Seniors receive a modest discount. All work comes with a full, written warranty.

Cheques, Credit cards

ABBA APPLIANCE REPAIR
3720 Savannah Ave (384-1003)
Hours: Daily 8 am. to 9 p.m. (see text)

Inexpensive repairs to appliances large and small (and parts sales) are the mainstay of this family-run business. They work from their home, so call ahead, or drop by "at a decent hour." They promise same-day service on most fridges, freezers and hot water tanks. With microwave ovens, they provide free pick-up and delivery.

Cheques

ABC ELECTRIC
831 Yates St (382-7221)
Hours: Mon–Fri 8:30–5:30; Sat 9–5

Likely Victoria's best source for small appliances, ABC is the approved repair depot for many name brands, including Braun and Cuisinart, though friends of ours found their repair work on the expensive side, so we stick to their sale items: Their Christmas sale revealed some incredible deals on Braun espresso machines, coffee makers, toasters and shavers. Another sale saw a cappuccino machine discounted to $189.99, down from $299.99. Other sales items have included Iona electric brooms, T-fal waffle and sandwich makers, Moulinex food processors, Black & Decker irons, Sunbeam steam valets and Cuisinart electric kettles.

Cheques, Credit cards

ASTRO BUILT-IN CENTRAL VACUUMS
Sidney: 11127 Tanager Rd (656-2122)
Hours: Mon–Sat 9–5:30

Claiming "wholesale warehouse-direct prices", Astro entices potential customers with free in-home demonstrations. We sense commissioned sales people, but they do have over 40 models and a number of accessories—and they've been in business since 1955—so add them to your shop-around list for prices.

Cheques, MasterCard

BILL'S APPLIANCE CENTRE
348 Burnside Rd E (386-2455)
Hours: Tue–Sat 9–5

Here's a place for new and fully reconditioned used appliances and parts. Bill specializes in General Electric, Inglis and Moffat, and will buy, sell and trade.

Cheques, Visa

BRUCE'S APPLIANCE REPAIR SERVICE
Address unavailable (727-7696; cel: 744-7710)
Hours: Call direct to technician at "any reasonable hour"

Bruce Martin has been in the repair business for over 35 years and is a member of the Appliance Service Association. He offers "guaranteed in-home repairs at honest prices" and works at a pre-quoted flat rate, so you know in advance what it will cost you. Seniors receive a modest discount.

Cheques

CAMCO PARTS STORE
479 Burnside Rd E (386-2488)
Hours: Mon–Fri 8–5; Sat 9–1

Everything is available here for do-it-yourself repairs (parts, accessories, advice from a friendly staff). They stock a complete line of multi-brand parts—genuine name brand parts—for G.E., Hotpoint, Moffat and McClary, and they fully warranty everything they sell. Seniors receive a modest discount.

Credit cards

COAST WHOLESALE APPLIANCE
761A Enterprise Cres (479-1223)
Hours: Mon–Wed & Sat 9–5; Th & Fri 8:30–9, Sun 10–5

This is where the builders shop for quality appliances at true wholesale prices; periodically, Coast runs a limited-time factory clearout of brands like Maytag, Norge, G.E., Sub Zero, Regency, Panasonic, White, Westinghouse, Modern Maid and Caloric. They carry ranges, dishwashers, fridges, washers and dryers, wall ovens and even tub enclosures. All appliances are fully guaranteed.

Credit cards

FUTURE SHOP (appliances)—See Audio & Video Equipment

LANSDOWNE APPLIANCE SALES & SERVICE
2517 Douglas St (383-1275)
Hours: Mon–Fri 8–5; Sat 8:30–5

There's a wide choice of rebuilt major appliances here, like fridges, stoves, washers, dryers and dishwashers. House calls for repairs, by the way, are charged at a modest flat-fee of $39.95 for one full hour.

Cheques, Credit cards

McFARLAND APPLIANCES
1917 Quadra st (383-8233)
Hours: Mon–Fri 8:30–5:30; Sat 9–5

When we were looking to furnish our new home here and would ask friends where to buy used appliances, they invariably referred us to McFarland. Over the years, we have bought a fridge, stove, dryer and basement freezer here—attracted at the time by their price tags (half the cost of new), pleased ever since by their performance. McFarland's appliances are reconditioned and tested (you're welcome to look at the performance-analysis printout), and guaranteed—parts and labor—for six months. The company seems so confident of its track record, it even makes available a photocopied "Guide to Buying Used Major Appliances," which you can take away and consult before shopping elsewhere. Not that *we* ever would.

Cheques, Credit cards

PHILIPS FACTORY SERVICES
D-493 Burnside Rd E (384-1169)
Hours: Mon–Fri 8:30–5; (Winter, add Sat 9–noon)

This is the official factory service outlet for all Philips appliances, and the company's other lines, such as Magnavox, Sylvania, Grundig—and they repair all other brand names as well. They are sometimes in on Saturday mornings in the summer, depending on their work load, so you can always call ahead if a weekend suits you better.

Cheques, Credit cards

RJ'S APPLIANCE REPAIR
740 Princess St (385-5345)
Hours: Mon–Sat 8:30–5:30

Here they buy, sell, trade and service all major brands of appliances, guaranteed used parts and all kinds of reconditioned appliances.

Cheques

RELIABLE PARTS
491C Burnside Rd E (381-5522)
Hours: Mon–Fri 8:30–5; Sat 8:30–12:30

Here's where we found that replacement knob for the dryer (at a small-change price). This 40-year-old business sells virtually any part for any make—exact replacement parts for all major appliances, plus service manuals. And if you've got a problem, call them or drop in for advice. Wheelchair accessible.

Cheques, Credit cards

SUPER DAVE'S USED STORE EQUIPMENT—**See Kitchen Equipment (next)**

T-T APPLIANCE CENTRE
1393 A Hillside Ave (361-2699)
Hours: Daily 8 a.m.–9 p.m.

They advertise low prices and low rates on all makes and models (new and reconditioned) of fridges, stoves, freezers, dishwashers, washers and dryers, plus in-home service throughout the Victoria area. All their work comes with a full written warranty. No extra charge for after hours, holidays and weekends. Seniors receive a modest discount.

Credit cards

THE VAC SHACK
2514 Douglas St (360-2514)
Hours:Mon–Sat 9–5

Here's the place for new, used and reconditioned vacuum cleaners at bargain-basement prices. They offer warranties of 3-month, 6-month and 1-year.

Cheques

VACUUM FACTORY
414 Craigflower Rd (383-2128)
Hours: Mon–Fri 9:30–5; Sat 10–4

Here they promise to fix all makes (one-day service on repairs) and they give free estimates before they begin work. Trades are taken on both new and used vacuums. Last time we were there, we spotted a vacuum special ($49), with power-head, $99.

Credit cards

WESTCOAST APPLIANCE CENTRE
Used: 602 Esquimalt Rd (382-0242; fax: 382-0178)
New: 608 Esquimalt Rd (382-5645)
Hours: Mon–Fri 9–5:30; Sat 9–5

Westcoast provides wholesale-to-public sales on new appliances and great discounts on used items. They claim to have "Victoria's largest showroom of new and reconditioned appliances"—and they sure do have lots of them. They'll buy your appliance, whether it's working or not, and everything they sell can come with an add-on one-year parts-and-labour warranty. Among the brands they carry are G.E., Whirlpool, Admiral, McClary, Danby and Magic Chef. They also do contract sales. Wheelchair accessible showroom. They'll offer 90-day interest-free financing O.A.C.

Credit cards, InterAc, Payment terms

KITCHEN EQUIPMENT, COOKS' SUPPLIES, CHINA, CRYSTAL & SILVER

Nothing pays bargain dividends quite like comparing prices and shopping the sales in the category of kitchen equipment, tabletop and cook's supplies. This category is almost a sure thing for gift inspiration.

AMSTEL METAL PRODUCTS
1–798 Fairview Rd (386-8244; fax: 386-5244)
Hours: Mon–Fri 8–4:30

Here's a source for new and used bakers' equipment—aluminum racks, bakery tables, restaurant and butcher equipment, coolers and display cases—and repairs on all kinds of kitchen and restaurant equipment.

Cash only

AVENUE CHINA & CHINTZ
1465 Hampshire Rd (595-1880)
Hours: Mon–Sat 10–5

Lost pieces of Grandma's china? The specialty here is discontinued china and crystal patterns, so you just might be able to fill out your set. Avenue also carries glassware, tabletop accessories, linens and small furnishings.

Cheques, Credit cards

THE CHINA CUPBOARD
1507 Wilmot Pl (598-3858)
Hours: Mon–Fri 10–5:30; Sat 10–5

Last spring, they moved just around the corner from their old location in Oak Bay Village, but they still buy and sell china, antiques and collectibles. There's usually a bargain table of clear-outs. Since they specialize in "discontinued china patterns from yesteryear," here's another good place to hunt for pieces to complete your set.

Credit cards

HOUSE OF KNIVES
Hillside Shopping Centre, 1644 Hillside Ave (595-1148)
Hours: Mon, Tue & Sat 9:30–5:30; Wed–Fri 9:30–9; Sun 11–5

B.C.-based and with a long history serving Victoria, House of Knives offers competitive pricing and a huge stock of knives, scissors, and other cutting instruments.

Credit cards

JEFFRIES AND COMPANY SILVERSMITHS
1026 Fort St (383-8315)
Hours: Mon–Fri 9–5; Sat 9–4

Once a year—usually in January—this posh shop offers English A-1 quality silver-plating at 25% off. All work is done by qualified silversmiths.

Credit cards

INTERNATIONAL KNIVES & DARTS (kitchen knives)—See Sporting Goods

KITCHEN CHARISMA
714 View St (384-8823)
Hours: Mon–Sat 9:30–5:30; Sun 11:30–4:30

The fall anniversary sale is worth waiting for: Reductions are 20–50% off regular prices on selected textiles, dishes, discontinued cookware, gadgets and bakeware.

Local cheques, Credit cards

KITCHEN ETIQUETTE
2018 Oak Bay Ave (598-3121; fax: 598-8291)
Hours: Mon–Wed & Sat 9:30–5; Th & Fri 9:30–5:30

Each spring, they have their factory-direct Paderno sale with huge

(40–75% off) discounts on all kinds of lifetime surgical stainless steel cookware. They run regular cookery classes, including Saturday classes for youngsters.

Credit cards

MING WO
547 Johnson St (480-0028; fax: same as phone)
Hours: Mon–Sat 10–6; Sun noon–5

Periodic sales punctuate the high-end look of Ming Wo. We found Lagostina cookware priced at 50% off, Calphalon all-clad cookware at 40% off, and wonderful, imported glassware and bottles at surprisingly low prices. Refunds are only given within 14 days, with your receipt.

Cheques, Credit cards

MURCHIE'S TEA & COFFEE
1110 Government St (383-3112; fax: 383-3255)
Hours: Mon–Wed 9–6; Th–Sat 9–9; Sun 10–6

The flagship store of this venerable tea and coffee company (dating from 1894, no less) has a whole back room devoted to a splendid array of china, flatware, teapots, cups and mugs, picnic baskets and so forth—some of which ends up on a clearance table at 50 to 60 per cent off. Seniors Day, every Wednesday, accords senior citizens a discount of 15 per cent on any purchase. Regardless of age, you get a free pound of Murchie's Espresso with the purchase of any espresso maker.

Cheques, Credit cards

ROBERT JAMES FINE CHINA
1005 Broad St (386-4588)
Hours: Mon–Sat 9:30–5:30; Sun noon–5

Though their everyday prices are too rich for our blood, their annual spring warehouse sale is nearly unbelievable, with savings up to 90% off. Rules are stringent: Stock is limited to first-come, first-served, all sales are final, there are no layaways and no exchanges. In-stock items only—the sale doesn't apply to previous reductions—and selection is limited.

Credit cards

SUPER DAVE'S ENTERPRISES
7210 Wallace Dr (652-3308)
Hours: Mon–Fri 9–5 (see text)

A great source for serious cooks, Super Dave's buys, sells, rents and leases-to-own all kinds of used food and used store equipment, including smallwares, ranges, grills, ovens (convection and standard), coolers, dishwashers, slicers and mixers, ice cream machines, vent hoods, stainless countertops, tables, chairs and booths, butcher blocks, weigh scales, wood and metal shelving, slat and peg boards, clothes racks, glass display cabinets, metal display racks and shelf-talkers, mannequins and storage bins. Their showroom at the Wallace Drive address (also known as Stelly's X Road) is a full 8,000 square feet. For weekend or after-hours appointments, call Dave at 477-3353. Mailing address (if you're seeking something in particular) is 1810 Cedar Hill X Road, Victoria V8P 2R4.

Cash preferred, Cheques "with reluctance"

DECORATIVE ACCESSORIES, UPHOLSTERY FABRICS & PICTURE FRAMING

There's lots of room for bargaining when seeking either decor accents or upholstery fabrics, particularly if you're prepared to look beyond the obvious sources, or enter the search without preconceived ideas about what will work where. Being open to "serendipity finds" really pays off. Picture frames are another story. There are a number of considerations beyond price alone when thinking of framing pictures. If the item is fine art, you may want to consider a method that will allow the best protection and preservation of the work, as well as the aesthetic concerns of suitable display. For children's artwork, you may be happy just to have it shrink-wrapped, or permanently bonded in plastic by a heat-process (usually a dry-mount press and plastic laminate). There are varying degrees of sophistication involved and a wide choice of styles. Among traditional framers, there is a wide variation in price. We have listed only those we hope will save you money, but we advise you to do some shopping around by phone first, especially if you've finally decided to frame several works at once; sometimes quantity orders will result in even better discounts.

ART BANK GALLERY
101 – 60 Bastion Square (380-0504)
Hours: Mon–Wed 9–6; Th & Fri 9–9; Sat 9–6; Sun 9–5:30

Look for Art Bank under the Polo Shop and watch newspapers for their regular coupons for 25% off your framing order. They also pledge to "match or better the savings on any competitor's special," and insist on a "no gimmicks" policy: "We won't be undersold."

Cheques, Credit cards

THE ART GALLERY OF GREATER VICTORIA
1040 Moss St (384-4101)
Hours: Mon–Sat 10–5; Sun 1–5

The Art Gallery runs free events at the AGGV for its Young Associate members ("YA brings people age 20ish to 40ish together with art") to promote an interest in art buying. The Gallery also rents fine B.C. art at a fraction of the cost to buy outright—and rentals can be applied to eventual purchase, if you decide you can't part with the piece.

Cheques, Credit cards

ART ON BROAD
1294 Broad St (385-94660
Hours: Mon–Sat 10–6; Sun noon–5

Specializing in decor accents and fancy glassware, Art on Broad nearly always has something on sale—like their periodic 50% off special on all glassware in stock.

Cheques, Credit cards

CALIFORNIA GLASS DESIGN
800 Blanshard St (383-1128)
Hours: Mon–Sat noon–5 (see text)

Though they close early at this shop across from the Cineplex Odeon theatres, they will arrange to see you during off hours by appointment. Among the offerings are charming period reproductions, recycled glassware (such as graceful candleholders for $26), reproduction Art Deco lamps (in many styles, from $59) and both etched glass and custom-etching available.

Credit cards

EASTERN INTERIORS—See Arts & Crafts Supplies

FRAME & SAVE
920 Johnson St (382-5012)
Hours: Mon–Sat 9:30–5:30

You'll save by doing your own framing and buying the necessary supplies at this factory-direct outlet. They also sell ready-made frames, canvases, posters and prints—at discount prices—and provide block mounting and custom framing services, too. Wheelchair accessible.

Credit cards

GLASS-SMITH (stained glass & art glass)—See Window Coverings

GLOBAL VILLAGE STORE (gifts)—See Alternative Clothing

ISLAND ART PUBLISHERS
Brentwood Bay: 6689 Mirah Rd (652-5181; fax: 652-2711)
Hours: See text

This wholesaler's annual warehouse sale is usually held around Hallowe'en (or the last Saturday of October), featuring close-outs, discontinued items, end-of-runs and marked merchandise priced from just $1. A second sale is sometimes added on the last Saturday of June. There's a good selection if you shop early on the one-day sale date. Among the goods are picture frames, mouldings, matboards, prints, posters, cards, matted pictures and framed novelty and gift items. The sale includes on-site specials and giveaways. Find them just off Keating X Road, next to Doorland. Watch for their newspaper ads or call ahead to determine the next sale date. Sale hours are generally on a Saturday from 9–4. Flyers are distributed to promote the event in the Brentwood area, so line-ups are not unusual. Out-of-towners can buy by mail order catalogue. Write to: P.O. Box 22063, Brentwood Bay, BC, V0S 1R0.

Cheques, Credit cards

JULIE'S COTTAGE CRAFTS
Market Square, 124B – 560 Johnson St (361-3885)
Hours: Mon & Th noon–4:30; Sat 11–4:30; Sun noon–4

Owner Julie Mah's annual clearance sale in the early spring features discounts of a modest 20–25%, but her everyday prices are low, considering what B.C. crafts sell for elsewhere.

Credit cards

LA BODEGA
566 David Street (388-6504)
Hours: Th, Fri & Sat 10–5:30

Promising "all pieces are directly purchased from the artisans", La Bodega bills itself as "an importer's retail outlet". Included in the stock—all at modest prices—are masks, candles, terra cotta works, planters, rustic (twig and bark) furniture, jewellery, charming folk art, functional and art glass, hand-woven textiles and unique lamps.

Cheques, Credit cards

THE MUSEUM SHOP
1011 Fort St (381-5553)
Hours: Mon–Sat 10–5:30

Periodically (often in January), the Museum Shop clears out its fine replicas at 25–50% off.

Cheques, Credit cards

NIEVAART GALLERY WAREHOUSE PICTURE FRAMES
Sidney: 9769C 5th St (656-2131)
Hours: Mon–Sat 9:30–5

Constant sales (such as their periodic 50% off metal frames promotion) reinforce the discount reputation of this Sidney gallery and frame shop.

Cheques, Credit cards, InterAc

ORIENTAL BOOK & GIFT SHOP
532 Fisgard St (385-2424)
Hours: Daily 10:30–6

This is as much a souvenir shop as a source for decorative accents. Among the deals are sandalwood soap (2 for 89 cents), toys, cheap sunglasses, wicker ware, some nice china and Chinese language cards.

Credit cards

OUT OF HAND GALLERY
566 Johnson St (384-5221)
Hours: Mon–Sat 10–5:30; Sun noon–5

Wonderful local crafts are displayed and sold here at Saturday-market prices. We found hand-crafted fountains, planters, bird-baths and other garden treasures on one visit, weavings and hand-thrown pottery on another—all at remarkably low prices, considering the high quality.

Credit cards

PICTURE PERFECT
University Heights, 324B – 3980 Shelbourne St (721-1313)
Hours: Mon–Wed & Sat 9:30–5:30; Th & Fri 9:30–9; Sun noon–5

A different special is on every month here, such as May: 30% off wood frames, June: 25–50% off art prints. Out front (facing into the mall) there's a 50% off bin of partial matboards and other discontinued items. Needlework workshops are a big drawing card here, too.

Credit cards

POTTERY PLUS
Sidney: 2428 Beacon Ave (656-7687)
Hours: Mon–Fri 10–5; Sat 9:30–5:30; Sun noon–4

Our friend, Ted Johnson, turned us on to this place, which sells the most remarkable hand-thrown, fired, gorgeous pots, bowls and planters at equally impressive discounts—about half what we'd expected to pay.

Cheques, Credit cards

QUONLEY'S GROCERY & COFFEE SHOP
1628 Government St (383-0623)
Hours: Mon–Sat 9 a.m–2 a.m.; Sun 9 a.m.–11 p.m

Once the only late-night convenience store in downtown Victoria, nowadays Quonley's is a cornucopia of souvenirs, pots, vases, Japanese paper goods & stationery, decorative iron baskets, greeting cards, rattan and wicker accents, mats, dishes and Chinese fans. And cheap prices! On the main floor are inexpensive stocking stuffers, party favours, candy, treats and imported Chinese condiments; downstairs are the large wicker and cane items.

Cheques, Credit cards

SIDNEY ANTIQUES & GIFT SHOP
Sidney: 2372 Beacon Ave (656-3621)
Hours: Mon–Sat 10–5:30; Sun noon–4

Considering the current prices of fine antiques, we counted ourselves lucky to have found this one, where there's a good choice of items—from desk-top to grand-piano-size—and prices are very reasonable. Last time in, we bought a simple yet elegant brass candle holder (for eight candles, like a *menorah*) for a mere $12. There are also numerous antique tins and other irresistible collectibles.

Credit cards

SMALL PRESSINGS GALLERY & PAPER
101 – 3 Fan Tan Alley (380-2479; fax: 388-7557)
Hours: Tue–Sat 11–5

A sweet and tiny shop at the edge of Fan Tan Alley, Small Pressings sells handmade papers at inexpensive prices. There's also modestly priced paper jewellery (more durable than it sounds), a free newsletter, and papermaking classes from basic to advanced.

Credit cards

STUDIO GLASS—See Window Coverings

U FRAME IT
2651 Douglas St (384-3444)
Hours: Mon–Wed, Fri & Sat 9:30–5:30; Th 9:30–9

This do-it-yourself framery saves you money two ways: First, you can obviously reduce costs by putting frames together (under expert supervision) yourself. Second, U-Frame-It holds semi-annual sales (typically early spring and fall) with 20% off their usual low u-do-it price and 20–50% off selected framed posters and prints. The store also offers custom framing at competitive prices.

Cheques, Credit cards

WAREHOUSE PICTURE FRAMES
207–3400 Douglas St (475-2273)
Sidney: 9769C 5th St (656-2131)
Hours: Mon–Fri 9–5:30; Sat 9–5

They seem to have something on sale almost any time: One month, it's 50% off all metal frames, the next off all wooden ones, any size, any frame (with complete custom-framing order).

Cheques, Credit cards

WILDLIFE CARVINGS
1756 McTavish Rd (656-1628)
Hours: Weekdays 9–5

J.F. Rickard operates a farmgate market selling his own, detailed wildlife hardwood carvings. He describes his pieces as "miniatures"—and his prices are small, too, given the workmanship: Birds range from $40 to $50, mammals (moose, for instance) from $60 to $70, and a Western theme will set you back $125 or so. They also sell farm-fresh eggs at bargain rates.

Cash preferred

WINNCRAFT WOOD PRODUCTS (home accents)—**See Furniture**

BEDDING, LINENS, MATTRESSES & HOT TUBS

Here's a category where shopping around for prices before you head out to buy—and studying newspapers and flyers—will always yield decent discounts. If you can bide your time and wait to purchase beds, pillows, bedding and linens, you'll always be able to get bargain prices during traditional "white sale" days twice a year: in early January (sometimes sales begin before Christmas) and early June.

One other caveat: Virtually every futon dealer claims to offer the lowest prices in town, so compare prices carefully and hold retailers to their claims

THE FOAM SHOP
2103 Douglas St (385-7622)
Hours: Mon–Th 9:30–5:30; Fri 9:30–8; Sat 10–5

Also known as "Thompson's Foam Shop", this place boasts Victoria's "widest selection of foam mattresses and toppers since 1979." Periodic sales present very low prices, although we've found their everyday prices among the best in town. They also carry quilts, pillows and foam wedges for back relief.

Credit cards, InterAc

THE FOAM ZONE
Town & Country, 4–3625 Douglas St (475-3255, 475-3626)
Hours: Mon–Fri 9–6; Sat 10–5

Boasts the "best foam prices in town," and they seem to deliver on the promise: A clearance table out front offered foam remnants starting at 50 cents. Friendly and knowledgeable staff on hand to help with mattress toppers, knee bolsters and convoluted foam. They can also advise on waterbed conversions and custom work for RVs and boats.

Credit cards

FORT STREET FUTONS
942 Fort St (381-3633; office: 361-1737)
Hours: Mon–Fri 10–5:30; Sat 10–5; Sun noon–4

In addition to the futon models, there's a nice selection of you-assemble-it pine shelving, plus unfinished pine boxes, dressers and trunks. Director's chairs run $29.95, and 100% cotton throws are $9.95. Don't miss the clearance box on the sidewalk, where items start at $1. Free delivery.

Credit cards

THE FUTON WAREHOUSE
106 Burnside Rd W (386-7032)
Hours: Mon–Th, Sat 9:30–5:30; Fri 9:30–8; Sun noon–5

This "futon factory outlet" and member of the Futon Association International shows off locally produced sofa beds, chairs, futons, frames, shelving, covers, traditional beds, foam toppers and even that great retro-item: the beanbag chair. They offer free delivery and on-the-spot financing (O.A.C.).

Credit cards

MHS DISTRIBUTORS
626 Esquimalt Rd (384-6311; fax: 384-7619)
Hours: Mon–Fri 8:30–4

This wholesale and retail operation caters to the hotel and motel industry and deals only in bulk, so canvass your friends and family before you call. Soaps, for example, come in case lots of 1000, but you can buy a minimum of six towels (white, brown or gold only). The best deal is the white, 100% cotton, 24x48-inch towels for $49.50 per dozen. Call for prices on beds, linens, laundry hampers and versatile pushcarts—just like the ones you see when you're checking out of a hotel.

Cheques

MAJESTIC FUTON & FRAME
2639 Quadra St. (361-3008)
Hours: Mon–Fri 10–6; Sat & Sun 10–5

Excellent prices on complete bed units (since many futon stores charge separately for frame and mattress). Singles with a basic foam core start at $159, doubles $209, queens $229; deluxe mattresses can take the still-cheap prices up to $279 (single), $329 (double), $349 (queen).

Credit cards

NORSTRAND
Mayfair Centre, 3147 Douglas St (380-6522)
Hours: Mon, Tue & Sat 9:30–5:30; Wed–Fri 9:30–9; Sun noon–5
Hillside Centre, 1644 Hillside Ave (370-5393)
Hours: Mon, Tue & Sat 9:30–5:30; Wed–Fri 9:30–9; Sun 11–5

Claiming the "widest selection of duvets in Canada," Norstrand recently opened a new store in Hillside Centre and celebrated with sales prices on feather pillows ($19.95), down pillows

($29.95) and goose down duvets (from $109.95); there's also a wide range of percale duvet cover and pillow sets in every size. Norstrand's stock is made in B.C.

Credit cards

ON THE SHELF
2950 Quadra St (383-6708)
Hours: Mon–Sat 10:30–5; Sun noon–5

Our friends Jan and James bought their futon and some shelving here after comparing prices all over town. Free delivery, too.

Cheques, Credit cards

PACIFIC LINEN
Mayfair Shopping Ctr, 3147 Douglas St (384-3377)
Hours: Mon & Tue 10–5:30; Wed–Fri 10–9; Sat 9–5:30; Sun noon–5

Though prices are often better at department store sales, the quality here is consistently high, and their sale prices exceptional. They feature sheets, comforters, accessories, household linens and a plethora of towels. Their credos: "No one sells for less," "The best prices in town," and "hassle-free return policy." Indeed, their guarantee states that their price will be "as low as or lower than all competitor's sale price for 60 days from date of purchase," and that they will refund the difference if you spot a lower price and bring in your original receipt. Recent sales have offered such deals as: 50% off 100% cotton print flannel sheets; buy-one-get-one-free print and quilted toss pillows; $19.99 for standard-size polyester or feather & down pillows; and $14.99 for 180 thread blended queen or king sheets. Gift certificates available.

Cheques, Credit cards

STATEWOOD SLEEP & SPA
3005 Douglas St (480-0966)
Hours: Mon–Wed & Sat 10–6; Th & Fri 10–9; Sun 11–5

An interesting conjunction of relaxation devices—beds and hot tubs—at what the store claims are the city's "guaranteed lowest prices." Futons and waterbeds start at $199, and there's a selection of low-priced oak and pine bedroom suites. If you don't dally, you can park free at Canadian Tire across the street.

Credit cards

SUPER CHANCE DISCOUNT
435 Simcoe 9385-2523)
Hours: Mon–Sat 9:30–5:30

Here's a shop that's not quite sure what it wants to be: Is it a garage sale outlet? Is it a linens and tabletop store? Is it a consignment shop? Well, actually, it's all of the above. At the front of the store, the dominant theme is new and somewhat discounted linens: Shelves of woven placemats, pillows, cotton throw rugs, bed linens, tablecloths, oven mitts and more. Along the walls and toward the back there are used sewing machines, small night-tables, kitchen chairs, utensils—all at thrift store prices. These are the consigned goods, which you are invited to bring in for assessment, rather than hold a garage sale. Consigned goods are received Wednesday to Saturday from 10 to 4 only.

Credit cards

THOMPSON'S FOAM SHOP—See THE FOAM SHOP, above

UNIVERSITY FUTONS
915 Fort St (381-4575)
Hours: Mon–Fri 10–5:30; Sat 10–5; Sun noon–4

This shelving-and-futon outlet has the distinction of carrying lovely pine window boxes, as well as their traditional pine bed frames (nicely finished, we might add) and a good assortment of shelving and shelf systems. They also sell coffee and end tables.

Credit cards

VINTAGE HOT TUBS
2000 Government St (382-7727; toll free 1-800-661-7727)
Hours: Mon–Sat 10–4:30; Sun noon–4

Periodically, this hot tub outlet clears out its inventory of home spas—and throws in incentives like two-for-one Hawaiian vacations. Additional incentives for early birds. Free one-year layaway. For inquiries from out of town, dial 1-800-661-7727, toll-free.

Cheques, Credit cards

WOODPECKER FUTONS (accessories and pine furniture)—See Furniture

CLEANING SUPPLIES

Please also see the section called "Cosmetics, Perfumes, Beauty & Grooming Supplies" for other home cleaning products not listed here.

ACME SUPPLIES
2311 Government St (383-8822)
Hours: Mon–Fri 8–4:30

We were tipped off to this place by one of their competitors, which suggests they enjoy good word-of-mouth support. The focus here is on janitorial and cleaning supplies, with best buys including their one gallon-size floor cleaner (about half what you'd pay for a smaller size, retail) and their tiny hotel soaps, which must be bought in case lots of 1,000.

Credit cards

DUSTBANE JANITORIAL SUPPLIES
577 Bay St (380-1666; fax: 381-5694)
Hours: Mon–Fri 8–4

Here's another source for bulk cleaning supplies, at strictly wholesale prices—about 50% off retail.

Cheques, Visa

JANITORS' WAREHOUSE
3342 Oak St (475-2443; fax: 475-2463)
Hours: Mon–Fri 8–5; Sat 9–1

Formerly owned by the Vancouver company of the same name (but sold to owners on the Island), this wholesale outlet stocks a vast array of cleaning materials and products. This is what the professionals use, and stock is priced to save you money (although many items are sold only in large quantities). Included are floor cleaners, furniture polish, laundry detergents, window-cleaning equipment and supplies, waxes, strippers/sealers, lint-free towels and commercial vacuum cleaners. Both new and used equipment can be bought or rented.

Cheques, Credit cards

SHAKLEE (cleaning supplies)—See Cosmetics

SOAP EXCHANGE
Town & Country, 3569 Douglas St (475-0033)
Hours: Mon–Wed & Sat 9:30–6; Th & Fri 9:30–8; Sun noon–5

"Welcome to a Cleaner World" is the heartfelt motto of this place near Wal-Mart, where you can buy concentrated soap refills for laundry, bathroom, kitchen and bath use for a fraction of what you'd pay for alternatives. (Inside the store, see the extensive accounting of their products compared in price to standard supermarket items. Savings work out to from 10% to 40% off retail.) The products are 100% Canadian-made and biodegradable, and the containers can be recycled. In fact, bring back the container and they'll replace it with another, but charge you only for the contents. The gamut of products runs from glass cleaner to shampoo to fabric softener.

Credit cards

GARDENING: NURSERIES, GARDEN SUPPLIES, MOWER REPAIRS & FLORISTS

ANNE'S FLOWERS BY DESIGN
1887 Oak Bay Ave (592-2110)
Hours: Mon–Fri 9:0–5:30; Sat 9:30–5

According to our super shopping sleuths Marilyn and Cary, this florist—besides being extraordinarily accommodating and reasonable in her prices—carries a wide array of "perpetual" arrangements and offers additional savings during seasonal sales. Owner Anne Domeij also makes beautiful wreaths and living arrangements, again at modest prices.

Credit cards

BIG BARN—See Produce, Eggs & Dairy Products

BORDEN MERCANTILE (garden utensils)—See Pets

BRENTWOOD BAY NURSERIES
Brentwood Bay: 1395 Benvenuto Ave (652-1507)
Hours: Mon–Sat 9–5; Sun 10–5

Behind Butterfly World, you'll find this nursery, which specializes in large bud, miniature roses and other decorative plants. They offer periodic specials on virtually everything in their stock, so watch local papers for ads.

Cheques, Credit cards

CANNOR NURSERY & FLORIST
4660 Elk Lake Dr (658-5415, 658-5057)
Hours: Daily 9–5:30

The deal here is ready-to-use 20-20-20 fertilizer, absolutely free. You pay $2 for the deposit on a four-litre container, and you may return as often as you like to refill it with fertilizer. At the end of the season, you can even return the container to have your deposit refunded. No purchase is necessary (although, of course, you'll be tempted to peruse the extensive nursery stock while you're there), and there's no limit to the fertilizer offer. Cannor has a huge selection of fruit trees, shade trees and ornamentals.

Cheques, Credit cards

CEDAR HILL NURSERIES AND GARDEN CENTRE
1550 Church Ave (477-2658)
Hours: Mon–Sat 9–5:30; Sun 10–5

We've found some of the best prices in the region at this garden centre—which has been serving Victoria gardeners for 40 years; consider bare root #1 grade roses from $5.49 each. Cedar Hill has both bush roses and climbers, and all are guaranteed to bloom the first summer. There's a host of other nursery stock, from azaleas to zinnias, and new arrivals showing up constantly. Find them behind McDonalds off Shelbourne (easy parking). Watch newspapers for special discounts.

Cheques, Credit cards, InterAc

DANICA NURSERIES
Saanich: 6705 Patricia Bay Hwy (652-2718)
Hours: Mon–Fri 8–4:30; Sat & Sun 9–4:30

There's almost always a sign up near the highway announcing 20% off bedding plants or similar nursery items, and their constant offer is for consumers to buy direct from the grower. Indeed, we've found the prices very low on their complete line of nursery stock, and Danica will also offer volume discounts—virtually wholesale prices—on all sorts of items bought in quantity.

Cheques, Credit cards

DIG THIS
Broadmead Village, 390-777 Royal Oak Dr (727-9922; fax: 727-9996)
45 Bastion Sq (385-3212)
Sidney: 9779 Fifth Ave (655-1400)
Hours: Mon–Sat 9:30–5:30; Sun noon–5

Dig This tends toward rather high-end "gifts and gear for gardeners," but the two shops also have clearance tables where something's always on sale. These are great stores for browsing, and the perfect places to choose a gift for your favourite gardeners.

Credit cards

ELK LAKE GARDEN CENTRE
Saanich: 5450 Patricia Bay Hwy (658-8812)
Hours: Daily 9–5:30

For more than two decades, we've been driving out to this garden centre, where there's always something wonderful on sale. You'll find inexpensive and hearty roses, perennials, bedding plants, trees, decorative plants and novelty items in a lovely setting right next to Elk Lake.

Cheques, Credit cards

FLOWERS ON TOP
1005 Broad St (383-5262)
Hours: Mon & Sat 10–6; Tue–Fri 8–6

Their ads promise "super bouquets, super selection, and super prices" and that's just what they deliver. And they actually do delivery. This is a florist, not a nursery, yet their prices are down to earth.

Credit cards

GARDEN WORKS
4290 Blenkinsop Rd (721-2140)
Oak Bay: 1916 Oak Bay Ave (595-4200)
Colwood: 1859 Island Hwy (478-2078)
Hours: Mon & Tue 9–6; Wed–Fri 9–9; Sat 9–5:30; Sun 9–5

Another place with seemingly constant sales; we've been particularly impressed with their tropicals, giftware and trees and shrubs. Look for good prices (via newspaper ads) in season on fertilizers and potted plants.

Cheques, Credit cards, InterAc

GROWERS DIRECT FRESH CUT FLOWERS
3789 Quadra St (383-5116; fax: 383-2154)
1241 Esquimalt Rd (389-0110; fax: 389-1521)
205-3749 Shelbourne St (721-1992)
Hours: Mon–Fri 9–6; Sat 9:30–5; Sun noon–4

Unbeatable prices for roses (sometimes as little as $9.95 a dozen) and other cut flowers set these shops apart—and account for their volume in sales. The Shelbourne location also offers classes in flower arranging and a full selection of dried and silk flowers. Additional discounts are available for volume orders, and they advertise special "business rates."

Credit cards

HAPPY VALLEY HERBS
Langford/Colwood: 3497 Happy Valley Rd (474-5767)
Hours: Wed–Sun 12:30–5

Lynda Dowling began the work of establishing Happy Valley Herbs in 1983 by clearing a paddock area on the old family farm to keep deer out. Today, on the site of what used to be her grandmother's goat pasture—about 35 minutes from downtown Victoria—she raises three acres of herbs, edible flowers and display gardens, open to the public from April 1 through October 1. She makes the largest part of her income by selling fresh herbs to local restaurants and flowers to Victoria florists, but during the months the farm is open (note hours above), you can buy herb plants, fresh-cut herbs, dried herbs and everlastings at farm-direct prices. On the second Sunday in July, Lynda hosts her annual "Lavender Day," when everyone is welcome to watch or help take wheelbarrow loads of the fragrant herb to the drying shed to be hung up. Throughout the summer, Lynda holds inexpensive workshops on edible flowers, and craft events on topics such as woven floral wreaths and tiaras. We were tipped to this hidden treasure by broadcaster Helen Pearce, who raved about the setting and the bargains.

Cheques

HARRY'S FLOWERS & GROCERIES
1802 Cook St (388-6498)
Hours: Daily 9–9
1817 Oak Bay Ave (598-3911)
Hours: Mon–Sat 9:30–8; Sun 10–8

We find the manager at the Cook Street store unnecessarily gruff, but you can't beat his prices: fresh roses at $7.95 a dozen, freesia bundles at $2.95 and long-stem roses for $12.95.

Cash

ISLAND SEED CO LTD
813 Darwin Ave (475-0144)
Hours: Mail order—See text

Their fine, locally grown seed is available at places you'd typically expect to see it: Garden Works, Capital Iron, Elk Lake, Tanner's, Big Barn—and it is selected to flourish in our coastal climate. They feature both flower and vegetable seeds and an ever-expanding herb list, plus a number of pest and insect repellants. The deal is that you can order from them via mail at prices generally below retail; write owner John Beatty at P.O. Box 4278, Depot #3, Station A, Victoria, V8X 3X8. Really nice folks, too.

Cheques

LE COTEAU FARMS
304 Walton Place (658-5888)
Hours: Daily 9–4:30

Since 1956, this family-owned and -operated business has allowed you to "buy direct from the grower." Le Coteau has offered incredible prices on healthy-looking fruit trees (a great selection of dwarf and semi-dwarf varieties), plus over 20 varieties of ornamentals. They even offer free pruning. Quantity discount are always available for large orders, so if you're planning to put in a small orchard, here's the place to shop. We also find their prices for hanging baskets and bedding plants exceptionally good, and there's a wide assortment of herbs. Find them off Oldfield Road, and tell owners Jacques and Marianne Ponchet (and son Daniel) that we sent you.

Cheques

LOU'S LAWNMOWER SERVICE
Vic West: 157 Langford St (385-2714)
Hours: Mon–Fri 8–5:30; Sat 9–1

You might think this entry is a little out of place, but you have to have your mower sharpened sometime—and here's the place to get a good job done cheaply.

Credit cards

MARIGOLD NURSERIES
Saanichton: Lochside Dr (652-3312; fax: 652-1330)
Hours: Daily 8–5:30

Laura Planes and Angela Ingram are among the eager and friendly greenhouse workers who keep this large operation ticking. The huge greenhouse is full of tropical plants, bedding plants, nursery stock and vegetable flats—all sold at grower-direct prices.

Cheques, Credit cards, InterAc

MILLSTREAM NURSERIES & GARDEN CENTRE
2412 Millstream Rd (478-2412)
Hours: Daily 9–5:30 (later during summer)

Over 90 varieties of roses are available at Millstream, with the emphasis on varieties that do well in West Coast gardens. Rhodos are well-priced from $5.95, and their extensive selection of fruit trees starts at only $13.25 (including tax).

Cheques, Credit cards

OLD-FASHIONED FLOWERS
738 Johnson St (384-3385, 384-4553)
Hours: Mon–Fri 9–5; Sat 10:30–2:30

Owner Denyce offers unusually good, personal service, which—added to her low prices—woos customers and guarantees repeat business. She also offers free delivery and 24-hour service, and she provides the rare service of preserving wedding flowers. Denyce is also known for her follow-up: One year after you've ordered a bouquet, she'll call to ask if you wish to send another birthday or anniversary remembrance. She stocks a wonderful assortment of wired ribbons and funky baskets, too.

Cheques, Credit cards

RED BARN FARM MARKET—See Produce, Eggs & Dairy Products

U.VIC PLANT SALE
McKinnon Gym at U.Vic (see text for phone)
Hours: See text

The University's spring plant sale is held in the McKinnon Gym from 10 am to 1 pm on the sale date, which is usually announced in tiny newspaper ads (or community calendar listings) sometime in March. For complete details, call Ken Ferris at 721-7638. The sale is operated by Finnerty Garden Friends as a fund-raiser, and there's a wide selection of shrubs, perennials, annuals and specialty plants all at rock-bottom prices. Line-ups are common, so plan to arrive early—and bring your own boxes.

Credit cards

VAN ISLE BRICKLOK
893 Van Isle Way (478-5012)
Hours: Daily 8–5:30

Free seminars are given as an inducement to get consumers into doing their own brick and stone walkways and retaining walls, but the bargain aspects we like best about Van Isle are the screened top soil, bark nuggets, bulk peat moss and cow manure you can buy here at near-wholesale prices. There's even free delivery on full truck-loads (share with a neighbour?) and expert advice on all manner of garden challenges.

Cheques, Credit cards

VICTORIA CACTUS & SUCCULENT SOCIETY
Pearkes Recreation Centre, 3100 Tillicum Rd
(655-3037, 388-9869)
Hours: Call for sale dates

The Society's "Cactus Carnival" features many of the more than 1,000 varieties of cactus grown worldwide, and this group is as avid about growing them for fun as they are about selling them at bargain prices to win new fans. The admission price is usually $2.50. Many of the cacti and succulents for sale are unique or hard to find. The hours are usually Saturday 10 am to 9 pm and Sunday 9–5.

Cash preferred

VICTORIA COMPOST EDUCATION CENTRE
1216 North Park St (386-9676, 386-9656)
Hours: Wed–Sat 10–5

Low-cost workshops are held here Wednesday evenings and Saturday afternoons; learn about composting, worm farming (save money and raise your own?) and organic farming. It's a non-profit project of the Fernwood Community Association and a great resource for the serious home gardener. Pre-register for workshops; fee is $3 for each subject.

Cheques

NOTES:

8. OFFICE NEEDS

OFFICE FURNITURE, MACHINES & SUPPLIES

ACCESS WEST RECYCLING CORP & CANADIAN LASER PRODUCTS

18 – 755 Vanalman Ave (479-1177)

Hours: Mon–Fri 8:30–5

Two branches of the same company operate at this address, providing similar services in recycling office toner cartridges for office machines, like printers and photocopiers. These are available here for an average price of $79—about 50% off new. Okidata remanufactured drum units are on hand, as are "remanufactured" laser printers, facsimile and photocopier supplies, ribbons and ozone filters. They also offer machine cleaning services, free delivery, printer servicing and low prices.

Cheques

COLUMBIA TYPEWRITER CENTRE (rentals, supplies, new & used)—See COLUMBIA OFFICE AUTOMATION in next section

GRAHAM SUPERIOR OFFICE MACHINES
1645B Fort St (598-2144, 598-5154; fax: 598-6079)
Hours: Mon–Fri 9–5

Economy IBM typewriter rentals (plus rent-to-own plans), IBM-trained sales and service and discount office supplies are the deals here. Very accommodating—the owner will come in on a Saturday or make an appointment to suit your schedule, if necessary.

Cheques, Credit cards

OFFICE DEPOT
755 Finlayson St (385-0001, 1-800-685-8800; fax: 1-800-685-5010)
Hours: Mon–Fri 8 a.m.–9 p.m.; Sat 9–7; Sun 10–6

Office Depot is right across from Mayfair, with its own, generous, parking lot. They claim you can save up to 75% on office supplies; indeed their flyer prices are often nothing short of amazing. We've bought such items as office chairs, a fax machine, storage units, a nice leather briefcase, tape, post-it notes and school supplies here, and have always felt we got the lowest prices in town. Good after-sale service, too, and they'll sell by mail order and fax.

Credit cards, Business accounts (O.A.C.)

RIBBON-X
2–2553 Quadra St (384-8795)
Hours: Mon–Fri 10–5

Here's another source for recycled office products, such as recycled ribbon and toner cartridges—save about 50% compared to buying new. They provide free pickup and delivery and will invoice you (O.A.C.) at delivery time (pay within 90 days).

Cheques, Credit cards

TYPE 'N WRITE SHOP
2713 Quadra St (381-4514; fax: 381-5821)
Hours: Mon–Fri 9–5; Sat 10–4

Formerly known as Victoria Typewriter, this place offers "everything for typing and writing." It's also the authorized warranty dealer for many brands of both electronic and manual machines. They sell new and used computers and word processors, provide rentals, accept trade-ins, and even offer photocopying, stationery and fax services.

Cheques, Credit cards

COMPUTER HARDWARE & SOFTWARE

COLUMBIA OFFICE AUTOMATION

748 Fort St (383-6751; fax: 384-8002)

Hours: Mon–Fri 9–5:30; Sat 9–5

This home and office computer company (with 20 years of local history) holds an annual clear-out sale with complete computer systems (monitor, enhanced keyboard, software and two-year warranty) at substantial savings. Other times of the year, they accept trade-ins, provide rentals, sales of new components, support service and repairs.

Credit cards

COMPUTASK

208 – 2614 Bridge St (389-6144)

Hours: Mon–Sat 9–5

Their reconditioned computers are sold in like-new condition, at prices you'd expect to pay for used. Free delivery and installation, upgrades and service.

Cheques, Credit cards

COMPU LEASE COMPUTER RENTALS

736 Caledonia Ave (388-7114; fax: 388-7799)

Hours: Mon–Fri 9–5:30

In addition to reasonable computer (IBM compatible and MacIntosh) rentals—by hour, week or month—they'll do laser prints for $1, photocopying for 10 cents (or less) per sheet and computer tutorials for $40/hr. Computer rentals start at $10 an hour, and their "shop rate" is $40.

Cheques, Credit cards

LAWRENCE EDDY BOOKS (software & used computers)—**See Books**

LONDON DRUGS

127 – 3995 Quadra St (727-2046; fax: 727-2096)

201 – 911 Yates St (381-4112; fax: 381-3638)

1907 Sooke Rd (474-2431; fax: 474-0954)

Hours: Mon–Wed & Sat 9–8; Th & Fri 9–9; Sun 10–6

London Drugs' computer prices are competitive with any in town —in fact, they'll meet or beat any of their rivals' advertised prices. Sale prices for peripherals, bulk paper and diskettes are worth waiting for.

Cheques, Credit cards

TESSERACT COMPUTER SYSTEMS & SOFTWARE

City Centre, 204 – 1483 Douglas St (382-3475; fax: 386-2515)

Hours: Mon–Fri 9–5:30; Sat 9–5; Sun 11–5

With more than a decade serving Victoria residents' computer needs, Tesseract has built a reputation for personal service and competitive prices. We've found their advertised specials to be really good value and their repair and support service excellent.

Cheques, Credit cards, InterAc

VANCOUVER ISLAND COMPUTER SHOW & SALE

Pearkes Recreation Centre, 3100 Tillicum Rd (388-6664)

Hours: Generally Sat & Sun 9–5

The annual computer sale and show is usually held in the spring, but there may be plans to run it more often, so call the Rec Centre for details on upcoming dates. We've found these shows a great way to pick up literature, try out new products and get deals. Some exhibitors will sell off their demo stock at the end of the show at bargain prices.

Payment varies according to exhibitor:
Generally Cheques and Credit cards

PACKAGING MATERIALS, PRINTING, PAPER PRODUCTS & STATIONERY

A & R PACKAGING & SHIPPING SERVICES
303 – 3347 Oak St (475-3362)
Hours: Mon–Fri 8:30–5; open some Sats (call ahead)

Save money by doing your own wrapping and packaging with materials bought from this discount source. We found sturdy boxes, crates, stuffings, labels and tape—or for a nominal charge, they'll package and ship for you in custom foam packaging.

Cheques, Credit cards

BUSINESS CARDS ETC.
Hillside Ctr, 106B – 1644 Hillside Ave (370-1200; fax: 370-1332)
Hours: Mon, Tues & Sat 9:30–5:30; Wed–Fri 9:30–9; Sun 11–5

Special deals are offered regularly here, on business cards, or, for instance, the personalized photo calendar (made from 12 of your own photos—what a great Christmas gift) for $19.95 (regular price: $38). Small orders are their specialty.

Credit cards

CITY COPY CENTRE
754 Broughton St (384-3666; fax: 384-3671)
Hours: Mon–Fri 8–6; Sat 9–5

A great source for low-dough full colour laser copies, its recent sale prices ranged from $1.95 for 8½ × 11 to $3.90 for 11 × 17 sheets. Copies from transparencies cost $4.95. Laminating isn't costly, either. There's a $10 minimum if you wish to pay by credit card.

Cheques, Credit cards (see text above)

DISCOUNT PRINTING
Sidney: 2367 Beacon (656-5325; fax: 656-5300)
Hours: Mon–Fri 9–4:30

An inexpensive source for custom rubber stamps, laminating, printing business forms, and photocopying and fax.

Cheques, Credit cards

DYNAPRINT
812 View St (381-3531; fax: 385-2623)
Hours: Mon–Fri 8–5 (some Sats—call ahead)

Our friend James thinks this is Victoria's best place for business cards: "Good . . . and cheap!" We found the full range of their pricing was affordable and their service fast and friendly.

Cheques, Credit cards

FOTOPRINT
975 Pandora Ave (382-8218; fax: 382-9952)
Hours: Mon–Fri 8–5:30

Here we found a business-card special of $16.95 for 500 and #22.95 for 1,000 (plus taxes). They do all kinds of office printing with free pick up and delivery and lots of free parking in their lot just opposite McDonald's.

Cheques, Credit cards

HILLSIDE PRINTING & COPY CENTRE
3050 Nanaimo St (386-5542; fax: 386-7838)
Hours: Mon–Fri 8–5:30

Short-run photocopying here is relatively expensive, but for large orders (with multiple originals) the price comes down to quite a bargain. Save 10% by running your job two-sided. Students receive a discount with student identification. Among the best deals here are cards and event tickets (cards from $27.95 for 100; tickets for $31 for 50), and their laminating runs only $3.50 for an 11 × 17 sheet.

Cheques, Credit cards

J & L COPY PLUS
777 Fort St (386-3333; fax: 386-3312
Hours: Mon–Fri 7–7; Sat 9–5

Here's where we found the best price in town for short-run photocopying—most types start at 9 cents a page (and go as low as 4 cents after 50 copies). They also rent computers (Mac or IBM from $10 per hour) and offer self-serve laser printing at flat rates from $1 for 10 minutes (no minimum). Laminating an 11 × 17 sheet costs $3, by the way. Super specials of the month are advertised via flyers in the store. Hemp paper is available for the environmentally conscious. Local cheques accepted.

Cash preferred

LAMINATE THIS!
Sidney: 9800 MacDonald Pk Rd (656-3927)
Hours: Mon–Fri 9–11 a.m., 1–4:30 p.m.

This place offers low rates for lamination and specializes in block mounting. Newly relocated at the end of what is now called Lysander Lane (where the new hangars are being built, but the street signs still say MacDonald Park). Follow MacDonald Park past where it used to end at Henry Ave, and Laminate This! is the last building on the new road.

Cheques

THE MARK-IT PLACE
107 – 733 Johnson St (383-3607; fax: 383-3647)
Hours: Mon–Fri 9:30–5

Here's the place for locally made, quality rubber stamps. Turnaround is really fast: Orders in by noon are ready the next afternoon. And their Trodat self-inking stamps are guaranteed for life—and can be recycled. You can order or get a quote by fax and they'll get back to you quickly. Free parking, right downtown.

Cheques, Credit cards

MONDAY CLASSIFIED ROLL-ENDS
1609 Blanshard St (382-6189)
Hours: Mon–Fri 8:30–5:30; Sat 10–5:30

Monday Magazine has a sideline selling (blank) newsprint roll-ends for anywhere from $2 to $10, depending on how much paper is left on the roll. These are perfect for kids' party tablecloths, banners, lining pets' cages, and lots of creative fun. Drop by anytime during normal office hours to see what they have on hand.

Cash only

NOTES:

9. MIXED BAG ("SUNDRY SALES & SERVICES")

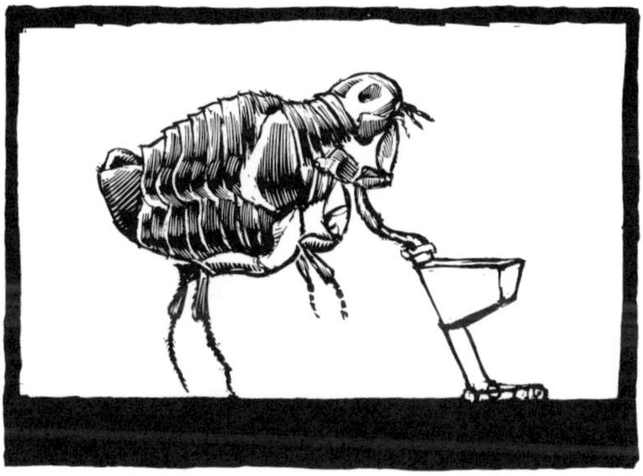

DEPARTMENT STORE-STYLE DISCOUNTERS

CONSUMERS DISTRIBUTING
Mayfair Mall (Blanshard Side), 305 – 3147 Douglas St (381-2434)
Hours: Mon, Tue & Sat 9:30–5:30; Wed–Fri 9:30–9; Sun noon–5

This big, Canadian source for consumer goods—everything from sporting goods to electronics to lawnmowers to barbecues to toys—does offer good sales prices, we admit, but we also find they are often out of the advertised special and we are forced to return with our raincheck several times to finally purchase the desired item. Their policy states: "Show us a lower advertised price... we'll beat it by 5% GUARANTEED!"

Cheques, Credit cards

FIELDS
1420 Douglas St (386-7554)
Colwood: Colwood Plaza, 4–1905 Sooke Rd (478-5581)
Esquimalt Plaza, 1153 Esquimalt Rd (383-4229)
Sooke: Evergreen Plaza, 6660 Sooke Rd (642-4455)
Hours: Mon–Th & Sat 9:30–5:30; Fri 9:30–9; Sun noon–5 (all)

Low-end family clothing and linens are the main interest in bargain shopping at Fields. There's always a reasonable assortment of inexpensive flannel shirts, no-name denims, winter coats and family footwear. Housewares are priced for those just starting out (perfect for college kids wanting low-cost pots, pans, plastics, etc.) and their everyday prices for pillow slips, comforters and pillows are almost as attractive as their sale prices. End-of-season clearances are widely advertised in-store and by flyers.

Credit cards

KMART
University Heights, 3986 Shelbourne St (477-6902)
Hours: Mon–Sat 9–9:30; Sun 9–5

Unpretentious good value awaits at KMART on goods as diverse as video tapes, footed cake plates, toiletries and cosmetics, cleaning supplies, small hardware items, wallpaper, workboots, woollen socks, throw-rugs, watches (great seasonal clearance prices), family apparel, automotive supplies, video games, linens, comforters, and housewares. The pharmacy line is 477-8513 for prescriptions and medication inquiries.

Cheques, Credit cards

SEARS
3190 Shelbourne St (595-9111)
Hours: Mon, Tue & Sat 9:30–5:30; Wed–Fri 9:30–9; Sun noon–5

A standard Sears store. The highlights are Kenmore appliances (washers and dryers are made for them by Inglis), low-end sportswear, beds and bedding (comforters, pillows and linens are particularly good values everyday), cosmetics and electronics. Corporately, Sears is trying very hard to move "up-market" and as they redesign and restock each store, they're getting closer to that goal—not there yet in Victoria, but for family budgets, Sears is still one resource to remember whenever you're comparing prices.

Cheques, Credit cards

WAL-MART
Town & Country Shopping Ctr, 3601 Douglas St (475-7585)
Hours: Mon–Fri 9 a.m.–10 p.m.; Sat 8–10; Sun 9–5

Wal-Mart has extended its hours since it assumed control of the former Woolco store at this location. The store itself was confusing around the time of the takeover, since so much of the old stock was being cleared out at up to 70% off regular retail, giving the aisles a junky, rummage sale look. Now, however, they've started to organize the new stock (which—surprisingly—closely resembles the old), so it's easier to move around the store and find what you want. We find excellent prices on health products, cosmetics and toiletries, family clothing and fabrics, and—though much of this stock is not to our taste—very competitive prices on furniture and beds. Wal-Mart is still our favourite place in Victoria to buy inexpensive mini-blinds. In fact, we bought a small one recently for under $3 (no lie)—identical to those we saw virtually everywhere else for three and four times that price.

Cheques, Credit cards

CHARITY RESALE & THRIFT SHOPS

BUY & SAVE FURNISHINGS
Sidney: 9818 4th St (656-7612)
Hours: Mon–Sat 9–5

Basically a high quality second-hand shop, this one has seasonal specials on clear-out items like "pre-owned" Christmas lights, collectibles, and even some quality antiques. There are reproduction antiques, used stereos and colour TVs, new brass headboards and complete brass beds, mattresses, kitchen tables, tools, electrical items, wall units, exercise equipment, sewing machines, and used books—cheap.

Cheques

BIBLES FOR MISSIONS THRIFT STORE
2520 Government St (479-3505, 361-9398)
Hours: Mon–Sat 9:30–5

This otherwise typical thrift shop seems to have its pricing out of step: Some quality items are dirt cheap while some dreadful knick-knacks are overpriced. All profits go to World Home Bible League, distributing bibles to countries where "there is a screaming need for the word of God." We found a whole box of girdles priced at $1.50 each (bras, 75 cents). There was a huge Hitachi microwave oven for $50, kitchen linoleum, stoves, ancient vacuum cleaners, lots of religious LPs (at 50 cents), a good selection of footwear, maternity clothing and outerwear. The store is very well organized. Want to donate or volunteer some time? Call 727-6952.

Cash only

JOE'S SECOND HAND STORE
Saanich: 1610 Island Hwy (474-2267)
Hours: Mon & Fri 10–5; Tue 10:30–4; Wed, Th, Sat 10–4; Sun noon–4

The owner of this place—in a strip mall next to Six Mile Market—is named Helen, even though it's called Joe's. Used couches, wooden and upholstered furniture, used beds and sofas here seem all to be in relatively good condition—and prices are rock bottom. Consider, for example, single beds from $49, double beds from $99 and sofas also priced at $99 and up.

Credit cards

GOODWILL
"Retail" store: 560 Yates St (385-5811)
"Save More" Store, Sidney: 9775 3rd St (655-3384)
Langford: 877 Goldstream Ave (478-5031)
Hours: Mon–Sat 9–5 (all)

Value-priced clothing, excellent selection, great buys on furniture, appliances, dishes and other housewares and cordial and helpful staff have all contributed to Goodwill's reputation as a reliable bargain source over the years. Also of note is Goodwill's gigantic book sale (50% off the already-low prices), which is held periodically, usually at the Langford location. Local ads announce their annual collectibles auction, held at their collection facility at 220 Bay St (near the bridge)—often early in November. Last year they offered more than 200 lots including fine china, jewellery, toys, linens, coins and silverware. A spring reupholstered furniture sale at the Yates St location is widely promoted via newspaper ads—save 35% off already low prices at that event.

Cheques, Credit cards, InterAc

PENINSULA COMMUNITY ASSOCIATION THRIFT SHOP
Sidney: 9783 3rd St (656-0134; fax: 655-4357)
Hours: Mon–Sat 9:30–4

Here we found typical thrift store fare, and well-organized, clean and neat. Good browsing and the potential for some real finds in small collectibles, pins and "junque."

Cash only

SALVATION ARMY THRIFT STORE
525 Johnson St (384-3755)
Sidney: 9775 2nd St (656-1732)
Langford: 2812 Bryn Maur Rd (478-6933)
Brentwood: 7177 West Saanich Rd (652-4622)
Sooke: Unit 3–6686C Sooke Rd (642-3612)
Saanich: 3948 Quadra St (727-3853)
Mill Bay: 855 Shawnigan-Mill Bay Rd (743-2123)
Hours: Mon–Sat 9:30–5 (most—see text)

So many locations, so little time. Please note that the Sidney store closes 12:30–1 Monday, Wednesday and Saturday for lunch, and that the Quadra St location closes at 4:25. All the Sally Anns have green-tag days, when daily selected clothing is half price. Every Tuesday is Seniors day (half price on clothing and linens). We find their furniture relatively expensive but the housewares and clothing very cheap. We're still using that great Proctor-Silex juicer we bought at the downtown branch for $10 a year ago. The Quadra branch is spacious, with a good selection on used books, shoes, housewares (better organized than most), furniture and replacement parts for electricals and machinery. The Sidney store has a lot of washers and dryers, etc. All come with a 30 day warranty (keep your receipt). Remember that no refunds are given at the Sally Ann, but they will give you a credit note or exchange if you have retained your receipt.

Credit cards

ST. VINCENT DE PAUL THRIFT STORE
840 View St (382-3213)
Langford: 2784 Claude Ave (478-0282)
Sidney: 9788B 2nd St (655-3188)
Sooke: 6661B Sooke Rd (642-7846)
Hours: Mon–Sat 9–5

Periodic sales of 50% off all items except furniture. We saw really nice cedar bird houses there recently—priced at only $10. The Sidney store is neat and well-organized, with great (low) prices. Several pieces of reupholstered furniture were particularly lovely—a wing-back chair and matching ottoman covered in an attractive brocade could have come from a ritzy shop. Here they were priced at only $375 for the set—about half to a third of what you'd expect to pay elsewhere.

Credit cards

THE THRIFT SHOP—ROYAL JUBILEE HOSPITAL
585 Johnson St (386-7111)
Hours: Mon–Fri 10–4; Sat 11–3

This shop is small and carries little stock, yet we've rarely come up empty-handed when we've gone in for a browse. It's another typical thrift store. Clothing is in very nice, clean condition.

Cash only

VALUE VILLAGE
1810 Store St (380-9422; fax: 380-9414)
Hours: Mon–Wed & Sat 9–6; Th & Fri 9–9; Sun 10–6

This huge store has such great scrounging possibilities that even our chic friend Deirdre told us not to overlook it for this book. "Not trendy," she said, "but lots of good second-hand clothing and books." Well, trendy is a relative term. Among the grunge-look teens we know, Value Village is very cool, indeed. This particular store is vast and though it has that distinctive thrift-shop odour, there is a huge selection of clothing, lots of furniture, modestly-priced bikes, books, records and bric-a-brac, and frankly, we hardly ever emerge without having bought something. Again, no returns, but they will give you a credit voucher if you bring the goods back promptly with your sales receipt.

Cheques, Credit cards

VILLAGE CRAFTS
2170 Oak Bay Ave (598-3822)
Hours: Mon–Sat 9:30–5:30

We've found the stock varies from ho-hum to fabulous at this retail sales outlet for many Oak Bay seniors who are talented knitters and crochet artists. And we do mean "artists"—some of their creations include clever finger puppets shaped like roosters, pigs, dragons and the characters from the Wizard of Oz. Sometimes we've found the most wonderful stuffed, crochet animals. There are usually carved items (cheap!), doilies and home-made jellies.

Local cheques, Cash preferred

W.I.N. THRIFT STORE—See Consignment

LIQUIDATORS, "GENERAL" & "$1.00" STORES

A BUCK OR TWO
Tillicum Mall, 31–3170 Tillicum Rd (381-1163; fax: 381-1193)
Hours: Mon, Tue & Sat 9:30–5:30; Wed–Fri 9:30–9; Sun noon–5

We like poking around this family-run dollar store because it has somewhat different stock than most of the other shops of its ilk: Candy, party decorations, fabric flowers, cleaning supplies, pet supplies, small hardware items and novelties—all at "a buck or two," as the name suggests. Good stocking stuffer or party favour source.

Cash only

CHINATOWN TRADING CO.
551 Fisgard St (381-5503; fax: 385-4771)
Hours: Daily 9–6; 9–9 in summer

Bill Harris has assembled an impressive assortment of Chinese imports, novelty items and decorative *chatchkas* in what would be a tourist trap, were the prices not so compellingly low. The huge store goes all the way through the block and sort of around a corner (you can enter the corner room from Fan Tan Alley, too). That small room, by the way, is transformed into a Christmas shop in the appropriate season, and continues to sell some small tree ornaments year-round, even when summer stock is expanded to include ceramic pots and wind chimes. Cheap beach mats were $1.79 (two for $2.99) and King Fu shoes only $2.99 when last we checked. Rattan baskets are at the front counter for your in-store use. Bins of children's novelties, party favours and stocking stuffers are neatly displayed as you enter off Fisgard St, and priced from a dime to 59 cents to $4. For instance, we found a bag of about 20 plastic dinosaurs for $3.99, paper kaleidoscopes for $1.49 and those irresistible tin pecking chickens for $2.49 each. Toward the back of the narrow shop there are tea sets, white and blue pottery soup bowls, Battenburg lace runners, pillows and shams, wind chimes (we liked the pig chimes for $4.89) and a whole museum-like tribute to the original Chinatown once around this site. Cheques accepted from local residents only.

Cheques (see text), Credit cards

DOLLAR STREET
CanWest Mall, 147–2945 Jacklin Rd (474-7945)
Hours: Mon, Tue & Sat 9:30–5:30; Wed–Fri 9:30–9; Sun noon–5

Virtually everything in this store is a dollar: Housewares, toys, spray bottles, candles, food, seasonal specialties (lots of Christmas, Easter and Hallowe'en stuff in appropriate shopping periods), and nice reproduction tins. Locator signs are shaped like street signs and hung from the ceiling, a cute extension of the street theme.

Cash only

DOLLARS WILD
Sidney: 2388 Beacon (656-1150)
Hours: Mon–Sat 9:30–5:30; Sun noon–5

3615 Shelbourne St (472-2077)

Hours: Mon–Th & Sat 9:30–5:30; Fri 9:30–9; Sun noon–5

The Sidney location is probably our favourite of all the dollar stores we've visited (including those on the mainland) because of the quality and diversity of its stock. We even bought an over-the-shower-head shampoo organizer for a dollar and later that week found its twin at Ikea for eight bucks. Other bargain goodies include stationery, housewares, spices, greeting cards, party supplies, gadgets and toys (as we said—better quality than at most). Friendly, informed staff. Excellent values throughout.

Cash only

GREAT CANADIAN DOLLAR STORE

University Heights, 3980 Shelbourne St (472-1846)

Hours: Mon–Wed & Sat 9:30–5:30; Th & Fri 9:30–9; Sun noon–5

This family-run business (friendly, helpful staff) offers stationery, housewares, greeting cards, candles, spices, inexpensive toys, novelties and stocking stuffers, craft and sewing supplies, and candy—all for about a dollar each. No refunds or exchanges.

Cash only

JUST A BUCK PLUS

652 Yates St (381-1130)

105–3995 Quadra St (727-6252)

Hours: Mon–Fri 10–6; Sat 9:30–6; Sun 11–5 (both)

The downtown location just opened in April, and they're already doing a booming business. We found the stock disappointingly low-end, but there were a few good deals: If you ever wanted to stock up on Barney the Dinosaur (and who doesn't?), they had a whole window display of the much-despised stuffed toys for $3 apiece. There's a children's play area in the window, too. Stationery, novelties, candles and party supplies round out the offerings.

Cheques

MINI-PRICE STORES
715 Pandora St (360-0888; fax: 360-0889)
Colwood Corners: 1905 Sooke Rd (474-7339)
Hours: Mon–Th & Sat 9:30–5:30; Fri 9:30–8; Sun 11–4

Self-described as "Victoria's general merchandise discount store," that sums up our take on this place. There are greeting cards at 60 cents each or two for $1, party supplies 70 cents to $1.95, housewares, stationery, cleaning liquids and supplies, bristol board and art/craft supplies, incense, spices, floor mats, cotton Dhurries and book remainders—a real hodge-podge of stock, but it's clean and neatly organized. A great browse. Self-serve photocopies are just 9 cents apiece (up to 20 copies); 21 or more cost 5 cents each.

Credit cards

SUPER CHANCE DISCOUNT—**See Bedding**

WAH YUEN GROCERY
534 Fisgard St (383-2813)
Hours: Daily 11–6:30

This Chinatown grocery sells inexpensive china, soup bowls, bamboo steamers, novelties, food, spices, tea, those hard-to-find Robertson jelly powders (for a bargain 69 cents each), handsome planters and incense.

Credit cards

SURPLUS & SECOND-HAND STORES

B.C. GOVERNMENT CASH & CARRY SALE
742 Vanalman Ave (744-4413)
Hours: Sale date 9–1

The Asset Investment Recovery Branch (how did we guess this was government-run?) holds periodic cash and carry sales at their new facility at the corner of Glanford and Vanalman Ave, including such items as desks, oak swivel chairs, filing cabinets, metal/wood shelving, bookcases, coffee/meeting tables, chalk/white boards, desk lamps, telephones, car stereos, stationery, bikes,

Zodiacs, computers, VGA monitors, printers and more. All items are pre-priced and may not be previewed before the sale date. Everything is sold on an "as-is, where-is" basis, which means no refunds if something mechanical is later found to be defective, and you must arrange to have large items moved yourself. The sale is not strictly "cash and carry," since major credit cards and bank-direct payment (debit cards) are accepted.

Credit cards, InterAc

D & S SECOND HAND STORE
Saanich: 4596 West Saanich Rd (479-1011)
Hours: Mon–Fri 10–5:30; Sat 11–4

This large store buys and sells used tools, furniture, appliances, garden equipment, fishing gear and complete estates. They offer: "Give us a call—if we don't have it, we'll try to get it!" A fairly wide selection of everything (when we were there last they had a surfeit of beds) at rock-bottom prices.

Cheques

JENKINS GOVERNMENT SURPLUS STORE
779 Pandora Ave (384-9799)
Hours: Mon–Fri 9–6; Sat 9–5

Desks, tables, chairs, chalkboards, projectors & screens, sofas and chairs, conference tables, computers (some are so old and huge that they look like they're cast offs from the original *Star Trek*), computer stands, filing cabinets, office dividers, storage cabinets, lockers, military clothing (and collectibles), boots, hats, coats, lab tables, wheelchairs, crutches, hospital beds—they've even had a working Zamboni in this large store. We find prices vary enormously: Some are dirt cheap, some make us think "What nerve!" At the back of our minds a tape is playing when we see the mountains of discarded government equipment at Jenkins, and it says, simply: "Your tax dollars at work."

Credit cards

JOHN'S MILITARY SURPLUS—**See Alternative Clothing**

KAY'S KORNER
337 Cook St (386-5978)
Hours: Tue–Fri 10–5:30; Sat 11–2

The sign says "experienced used goods," but our instincts say that these items are in pretty upscale condition. Prices are surprisingly low for such quality used small furnishings, lamps, decorative accents and a few hand-made crafts. In the Cook St Village.

Cheques

LAURA'S GENERAL STORE
Esquimalt: 550 Comerford St (360-2100)
Hours: Mon 1–5:30; Tue–Fri 11–5:30; Sat noon–5

Here they buy and sell small furnishings, housewares, toys and baby accessories. Laura will pay cash for most household items in good condition.

Cheques

LOMAS BARGAIN SHOP—See Furniture

ROGER'S TREASURES
3582 Quadra St (360-9036)
Hours: Mon–Fri 10–6; Sat 10–5

Here they buy "garage sale items," which means some of their sources hold their own garage sales and anything good that remains unsold can be carted over to Roger's. There are old trunks (well-priced), records for $1 each and cassette tapes and videos for peanuts.

Cheques

WEST COAST LIQUIDATORS
3948 Quadra St (479-1777)
Hours: Mon–Sat 10–5:30; Sun noon–5

Mark Brady runs this true liquidation outlet, which buys up merchandise from distress sales, estates, bankruptcies, close-outs and manufacturers' discontinued lines to offer everything under the sun: Housewares, tools, tarps, food and some clothing.

Cheques, Credit cards

AUCTIONS, SWAP MEETS, FLEA MARKETS, GARAGE OR COMMUNITY SALES

If you're after lowest prices on the best quality, handmade or collectible items, chances are you'll find them at local community fairs, charity thrift sales, or privately run garage sales. As we mentioned elsewhere, Victoria and vicinity is blessed with literally dozens of free, weekly (or periodical) newspapers and magazines—possibly more of these publications than you'll ever find in any other city, anywhere. Furthermore, these freebies are so liberally distributed around town, that there's hardly a street corner or crossroad that doesn't have three or four help-yourself distribution boxes standing sentinel on it. In fact, in the upper courtyard just off the Johnson Street entrance to Market Square, there must be eight or nine of them—all different, and all free.

Checking these publications for "community notice board"-type ads always reveals some weekend craft market, bake sale, rummage (or as the Brits say "jumble") sales, or a big swap meet. Goods offered could be anything from a hand-knit Afghan for a fraction of its worth to a full computer system at a factory-direct price. And the *Times-Colonist*'s Friday and weekend papers list a good many local garage sales and events. We like to circle the ones that sound most promising and work up an itinerary, because in this case, the early bird gets the bargoon.

We've written up the must-see ones in this chapter. And here are some of the other sales we've discovered: **Asthma Society Rummage Sale** (Stelly's High School, May); **Barnabas Church Rummage & Bake Sale** (Belmont and Begbie, periodic); **Bastion Theatre Committee Garage Sale** (periodic, location announced); **Daughters of the Nile Annual Bazaar** (St Mary's Church, 1701 Elgin, info 656-2023); **Edelweiss Club Yard Sale** (periodic—check club bulletin board at Conti Deli on Government St for details); **Esquimalt Kids Swap Meet** (Esquimalt Rec Centre—386-6128 for dates); **Cook Street Community Garage Sale** (380 Cook St, by Fairfield New Horizons—384-6542 for details); **Heart & Stroke Foundation Bridge and Auction Day** (Centennial Church Hall, 649 Gorge E—call 382-4035 for dates); **James Bay Family Centre Spring Tea** (18-435 Simcoe—361-9757 for details); **James Bay New Horizons Rummage Sale** (234 Menzies st—386-3035 for dates);

Kiwanis Village Annual Rummage Sale (Viv Shoemaker Centre, 1419 Mallek Cres—595-0331 for info); **Oak Bay Kiwanis Pavilion Harvest Bazaar** (3034 Cedar Hill Rd—autumn—598-2022 for exact timing); **Oktoberfest** (St David by the Sea Anglican Church, 5182 Cordova Bay Rd—autumn); **St. Luke's Church Spring Fair** (3821 Cedar Hill X Rd—spring); **Shalom Preschool Garage Sale** (periodic, 427 Government); **Theatre Society Costume Sale** (periodic, location announced); **Unitarian Church Plant & Bake Sale** (106 Superior St, periodic); and the **Victoria Rhododendron Society Sale** (usually at Cadboro Bay United Church Hall, 2625 Arbutus Rd—385-4302—spring).

Most auctions start precisely at the announced hour, and you are expected to have completed your credit approval and payment procedures prior to that time in order to get your bidding paddle. You should also have viewed the auction items in advance. And auctions are no place to wave at a friend across the room, by the way.

BUY & SELL
2001 Douglas St (361-1200—free ad line—see text)
Hours: Mon–Fri 9–5

One of the best ways to sell your goods, buy quality used items and advertise for things you *want* to buy, this newspaper offers free ads to sellers—or you can pay a nominal fee for a display or photo ad to attract a wider audience. For paid classified ads, call 361-1222, or fax 360-1407. The paper is published every Thursday; deadline for all ad insertions is 5 pm the preceding Monday.

Cheques, Credit cards (free ads no charge, of course)

COMMUNITY ARTS COUNCIL OF GREATER VICTORIA GARAGE SALE
1131 McKenzie St (381-2787)
Hours: See text

Everything from art supplies to "junque" is available at this spring event (usually held at the beginning of May) in their location near the Cook St Village. All funds go toward helping raise funds and community awareness about art, for their grants and awards/recognition for worthy artists and artisans.

Cash only

FARMERS MARKET (METCHOSIN PRODUCERS ASSOCIATION)

Happy Valley Rd near Metchosin Rd (phone unavailable)

Hours: Sun 11–2

Bedding plants, fresh produce and farm-fresh eggs are the main attractions at the barn on the Municipal Hall Grounds in Metchosin every Sunday from May through October. Watch for signs on Happy Valley Road.

Cash only

FERNWOOD VILLAGE SATURDAY MARKET

1200 block Fernwood Rd (389-0713, 480-1192, 386-5523)

Hours: Sat noon–4

Usually commencing in early May and operating every Saturday until Thanksgiving, this street market just off the intersection of Fernwood Rd and Gladstone Ave features food (mainly organic produce), clothing (lots of alternative attire), hand-crafted items, jewellery, psychic readings, entertainment and a lively, community atmosphere. It's held in the cobblestone courtyard of the Belfry Theatre and vendors (as well as purchasers) are always welcome to call for info.

Cash only

5 CORNERS FLEA MARKET

Langford: 721 Station Ave (474-2778, 382-6740)

Hours: Sat 10–4, Sun 8–4

This is the location of Victoria's largest indoor/outdoor, rain or shine, year-round flea market, with lots of antiques and collectibles.

Cash preferred

FRIENDS OF THE LIBRARY USED BOOK SALE

Sidney: 10091 Resthaven Dr (656-3956, 656-0944)

Hours: See text

This periodic sale runs on the announced day (call for next sale date) from 10 am to 4 pm (no early birds) at the Sidney-North Saanich branch of the Vancouver Island Regional Library—tons of used books for every interest, both hard and soft covers. Bring your own cardboard box to make carrying your booty a little easier

Cash only

GOODWILL
560 Yates St (385-5811)
Sidney: 9775 3rd St (655-3384)
Hours: Mon–Sat 9–5

Periodic book sales at these locations of Goodwill are where a boastful friend of our has discovered some first-class first editions for "bupkas" (peanuts).

Cheques, Credit cards

HIGHWAY AUCTIONS
Junction Trans Canada Hwy & Cowichan Bay Rd (743-3535)
Hours: See text

Auctions of special consignments are announced by this outfit (actual mailing address is RR 2, Cobble Hill) periodically in the press—or call to ask them what's on their auction schedule. Previews are held for a few days in advance of big auctions, and the auction itself is usually on a Sunday, commencing at noon exactly.

Cheques, Credit cards

KILSHAW'S AUCTIONEERS
1115 Fort St (384-6441)
Hours: See text

One of Victoria's premier auction houses, Kilshaw's accepts consignments for auctions, and previews its proferred goods for several days before the auction date—usually a Thursday evening, when the auction starts promptly at 7 pm. Items offered might be antiques, fine art, china, silver, crystal or collectibles—all of top quality.

Cheques, Credit cards

LUNDS AUCTIONEERS & APPRAISERS
926 Fort Street (386-3308; fax: 386-5469)
Hours: See text

Another long-established firm, Lunds runs various auctions on a regular schedule: Their household auctions are usually on Tuesdays at 1 and 7 pm, while their fine art and antique auctions are often slated for Mondays at 7 sharp. They appraise and accept your consigned goods only on Wednesday or Thursday (9–5) and will provide in-home estimates on request. Out of town inquiries, call 1-800-363-5863, toll-free.

Cheques, Credit cards

MOSS STREET COMMUNITY MARKET
Corner of Moss & Fairfield (478-6084)
Hours: Sat 10–2

This every-Saturday market features fresh, organic vegetables, locally produced crafts, clothing, jewellery, candles, bulk honey and children's entertainment, all in a kind of festival atmosphere—sometimes including clowns, puppet shows, magic and stories. All children's activities (when they have them) are free.

Cash preferred

OAK BAY TEA PARTY SOCIETY
2832 Cadboro Bay Rd (592-5119)
Hours: See text

This huge annual tea party is usually held early in June (it's been happening every year since 1962) and includes entertainment (dancers, musicians, jugglers), food stalls, crafts, baked goods, and of course, tea. It's all very proper, and it's worth the price of admission just to see the ladies' hats.

Cash only

PENINSULA COUNTRY MARKET
Central Saanich: Fair grounds, Stelly's X Rd (652-4024)
Hours: Sat 9–1

This weekly Saturday market is generally held from just after Easter, right up until Thanksgiving at the new fair grounds in Central Saanich. You'll find fresh produce (lots of it organic), bulk prices for honey and corn, and farm-direct prices. Free parking, free admission. Bring a cardboard box so your apples don't bruise in the trunk of your car.

Cash only

SIDNEY FLEA MARKET

Sidney: Sanscha Hall, Hwy 17 & Beacon Ave (656-4563)

Hours: Sun 9–4

There's a 50 cent admission charge to get into the sale, which occupies one large room and one smaller one in the hall. Call ahead to check times before making a special trip, as there has been some controversy about community use of Sanscha Hall, so location and hours may change. We found nice Indian jewellery, household items, bric-a-brac, fabric bolts, stamps, trading cards, old books, toys, collectibles, tools, hand-knits, children's wooden furniture, new and used clothing and homemade jelly. Stock changes from week to week, though there are some regular vendors. We found the best deals (and the same size crowds) on rainy days.

Cash only

TIMES COLONIST CLASSIFIED

2621 Douglas St (386-2121)

Hours: Mon–Fri 7:30–6; Sat 8:30–4:30

The T-C offers Thrifty ads at only 15 cents a word for householders who have inexpensive goods for sale. Each item must be priced to sell for under $199, every item in the ad must be priced, and garage sale ads or group sales do not qualify for this cheap ad rate. There's a minimum charge of $1.50 per day (plus GST), so if you are spare with your words, you can clear your attic out for pennies. Ads may be placed by phone.

Credit cards

UKRAINIAN DINNER

3277 Douglas St (475-2585)

Hours: One Fri 5–8 per month (see text)

Once a week, the Ukrainian Cultural Centre serves its now-famous dinner. Usually, it consists of a heaping plate of perogies, cole slaw, cabbage rolls, Ukrainian sausage and other Ukrainian delicacies—lovingly made by expert cooks among the Centre's members and offered at the wallet-saving (but belt-busting) price of $7. Proceeds go to benefit the Ukrainian Dance Club. Alcoholic beverages (like beer) cost an additional $2; a bowl of borscht with buttered Russian rye bread costs an extra buck, as do the home-baked desserts. If there's pie, it's $1.25. All told, you should be able to dine for under $10. The dinner is held the second Friday of every month—except for the months of December, July and August, and though there's a queue out front (seating for 160 people), you're usually in and served within 10 minutes. Our friend Marilyn says: "Here's the bottom line—quantity, quality, home-cooked food. How can you go wrong?"

Cash only

VARIETY FLEA MARKET
1600 Government St (381-5033)
Hours: Sun 9–2

This downtown flea market charges 50 cents for admission at the O.A.P. building on the corner of Pandora and Government. Tables to vendors are $10. We found a good selection of household goods and very friendly sellers—in fact, we got a terrific buy on a perfectly good Sunbeam Mixmaster (sans mixing bowl) for only $5. To that anonymous vendor: Thanks. It works great.

As we were going to press, this weekly flea market was interrupting its operations until the beginning of August, but they were resuming soon and planning to keep going year-round

Cash only

VICTORIA CURLING CLUB FLEA MARKET
Victoria Curling Club, 1952 Quadra St (386-6396; fax: 386-6390)
Hours: Sun 10–3

Operating sporadically (they close for summer holidays for the last two weeks of August, for instance), this is a typical flea market with used household goods, some handicrafts and some food in over 17,000 square feet of indoor space. Patio restaurant. Free admission. Free, ample parking.

Cash only

VICTORIA FLEA MARKET
3400 Tillicum Rd (656-6856)
Hours: Sun 8–2

Not to be confused with the downtown flea market, this one is across from Tillicum Mall and calls itself "Victoria's largest indoor flea market." It operates every Sunday, year-round. Sellers only may arrive at 7:30 am. Space for vendors may now be reserved by calling their info number for a table location. Goods for sale run the gamut from household items to new and used clothing, crafts, books, used tools and imported novelties.

Cash only

VICTORIA PARENTS OF TWINS & TRIPLETS ASSOCIATION
Location and phone: See text
Hours: Sun 10–noon

This group obviously has an overabundance of children's toys, clothing and furniture, since they've had to buy everything in two and threes, so their sales are a good bargain source for anyone with a growing family. Their sale is often held in the spring at the Oak Bay Scout Hall, and meetings for their members take place at G.R. Pearkes Centre, 3970 Haro Rd at 7:30 pm on the second Tuesday of every month. For information on upcoming sales events, call Sue at 744-1058 or Margo at 479-4305.

Cash only

WESTERN SPEEDWAY SWAP N SHOP
650 Hordon (474-2151)
Hours: Sun 7–2

This large swap meet features everything you'd expect: Household goods, clothing, craft items, furniture, tools, books and magazines—and low prices. Sellers pay $12 a table; buyers pay $1 admission.

Cash only

YM-YWCA BOOK SALE
Downtown "Y", 880 Courtney St (386-7511)
Hours: See text

This always eagerly-anticipated event takes place over two or three days every spring at the downtown Y. Sale time is usually 11–4 on the Saturday and 10–3 on the Sunday, although occasionally the sale starts on a Friday, so be sure to call in late February to find out when the next sale is scheduled. Folks start lining up by about 9 am on the first day and there are no early bird sales allowed. We saw a great many dealers there, pushing their way to the front and organized enough to have brought their own boxes, canvas book-bags and even one portable handcart—to make carrying books easier. Books are laid out on tables in a large room on the Y's second floor, and are categorized according to their value, so that you'll pay $1 to $3 for most, or cheaper rates for buying several of one "classification." The bottom line is, they're cheap —and there's everything from coffee table hardcover books to cheesy science fiction paperbacks to school texts to 80-year-old children's books. Worth waiting for. Free admission. Free coffee.

Cash only

MEMBERS-ONLY DISCOUNT CLUBS

ADVANTAGE EXCHANGE GROUP

P.O Box 5487, Station B, Victoria V8R6S4 (595-2810)

Hours: Machine answers 24 hours

A business to-business and buying club, Advantage charges $19.95 for one member and $14.95 for a second family member or business partner. After a year, if you don't feel you got your money's worth in this club, they'll refund your membership fee, no questions asked. They promise you savings of up to $5,000 through discounts offered by local merchants, restaurants, personal services, repairs, professional services and even cellular phones. A newsletter is sent periodically to all paid-up members, outlining new discounts and advertising current member services. The merchant info number (shown above) explains special offers and is updated regularly. Call to inquire about a free, four-month trial membership.

Cheques

MISCELLANEOUS SERVICES; SAVINGS/MARKETPLACE PUBLICATIONS

BUY & SELL (free ads)—See Auctions & Community Sales

CUSTOM CARE CLEANERS
Oak Bay: 2077 Cadboro Bay Rd (592-5326)
Hours: Mon–Sat 7–6

An early bird discount of 20% is offered to all patrons who drop off cleaning from 7–8 am. There's also a daily discount for seniors.

Credit cards

FOR SALE BY OWNER
5033 Cambria Wood Terrace (658-0156)
Hours: Daily 9–9

This service helps you sell you own home for a flat fee, far less than you'd pay a commissioned realtor. They supply a kit with various options, depending on how complex the sale of your home might be, and how much help you need to direct your own financial arrangements. The price range for the kits is $69 to $249. In addition, they run your listing in their catalogue for four issues—usually spanning about 60 days—and during that period they are more than happy to offer information handouts, advice and moral support. Their success rate for helping first-time vendors sell their home (on their first attempt) is about 42%.

Cheques

MEMORIAL SOCIETY OF B.C.
519–620 View St, Victoria V8W 1J6 (385-5214)
Hours: Mon–Th 9–2; summer: closed Fri June/July/August

Pre-planning your own funeral makes good, common sense, so that you'll save your survivors the additional grief of coping with decisions and expenses. The Memorial Society asks a lifetime membership fee of $10, then provides special contract funeral price lists which will save your grieving family as much as 90% off "retail" funeral costs. Add this to your living will—it's the thoughtful thing to do. During off-hours, new members can pick up application forms at First Memorial Services, 1155 Fort St (384-5512), which is open Mon-Fri 9–5. A free, no obligation brochure is available by phone, by writing or by dropping in.

Cheques

THE NATIONAL FOR SALE PHONE CO.
208 – 2187 Oak Bay Ave (595-2222)
Hours: 24 hours (interactive recorded message)

If you're planning to move to any major metropolitan centre in Canada, this advertiser-supported (but free to consumers) phone service supplies information on real estate and professional services in your destination city.

Free

THE SAVERS' & INVESTORS' GUIDE
316 – 1575 Begbie St, Victoria, V8R 1L2 (598-0878)
Hours: Call or write, 24 hrs

Publisher Janet Noden produces this monthly newsletter (since Dec '92) which is similar to the U.S.-based Tightwad's Gazette, except it's not quite so "down-home" and offers a fairly sophisticated approach to investment strategy, along with sage advice about saving money everyday. Cost is $24 per year.

Cheques

NOTES:

INDEX

T

ORDER FORM

Qty	Item	Amt
	Victoria on the Cheap by Anne Garber & John Keyes Victoria can be frightfully expensive—but not with this indispensible guide to discounters, deals, restaurants and classic British country pubs—in hand. ISBN 0-9695187-4-9	$10.95
	101 Uses for a Severed Penis by Dan Murphy Cartoonist Murphy turns his considerable wit and talent toward (shall we say) *sensitive* matters in this cutting-edge satire, proving the penis mightier than the sword! ISBN 0-9695187-3-0	$6.95
	The Vancouver Super Shopper by Anne Garber & Lorraine Gannon Everything (and place) you need to know to save money in Vancouver and environs: clothing, food, renovation, kids' stuff, factory outlets & more. ISBN 0-9695187-2-2	$12.95
	The Serious Shopper's Guide to Vancouver by Anne Garber & Lorraine Gannon District-by-district tours of the best shopping in and around Vancouver, with focus on the best, the most unusual or the cheapest! Includes detailed maps. ISBN 0-9695187-0-6	$9.95
	Cheap Eats by Anne Garber & Marv Newland Over 130 diners, greasy spoons, cafes, ma-and-pa eateries, cafeterias and other discount dining in and around Vancouver comprehensively reviewed and indexed for easy access. Illustrated. ISBN 0-965187-1-4	$9.95
	The Catalogue of Canadian Catalogues by Leila Albala Montreal author Leila Albala gives detailed descriptions of the best of Canada's mail order catalogues. Clearly indexed. Illustrated. ISBN 0-9219930-5-6	$9.95
	Easy Halloween Costumes for Kids by Leila Albala Our friend Leila has another winner in this book with over a hundred scalable costumes for kids "of all ages". Complete instructions; fully illustrated. ISBN 0-9691932-6-2	$12.95
	Subtotal	

See reverse for ordering.

SERIOUS PUBLISHING
7249 Waverley Avenue • Burnaby, B.C. • V5J 4A7
(604) 879-0321 • Fax: 875-0007

Subtotal	
Add 20% shipping & handling	
Add 7% GST (Canadian orders only)	
Total (cheque or money order enclosed)	
(American orders, prices in U.S. dollars)	

PLEASE PRINT

NAME ______________________________

STREET ______________________________

CITY & PROV/STATE ______________________________

POSTAL/ZIP CODE ______________________________

FAX (for info on new titles) ______________________________

Note: Payment by Visa to our fax #: (604) 875-0007. Please include your Visa number, expiry date, signature and print the name of the person to whom the card is issued.

"Serious" Phone inquiries: (604) 879-0321
Serious Publishing GST # R 127510964

For a complete list of available titles, see reverse.